Backpacker's Start-Up:

A Beginner's Guide to Hiking & Backpacking

By
Doug Werner

Photography by Doug Werner

Start-Up Sports **#10**

Tracks Publishing
San Diego, California

Backpacker's Start-Up:
A Beginner's Guide to Hiking & Backpacking

By Doug Werner

Start-Up Sports / Tracks Publishing
140 Brightwood Avenue
Chula Vista, CA 91910
619-476-7125   Fax 619-476-8173

Copyright © 1999 by Doug Werner

Publisher's Cataloging in Publication

Werner, Doug, 1950-
     Backpacker's start-up : a beginner's guide to hiking and backpacking / Doug Werner.
     p. cm. – (Start-up sports ; #10)
     Includes bibliographical references and index.
     Preassigned LCCN: 98-61173.
     ISBN: 1-884654-10-X

1. Backpacking. 2. Hiking   I. Title.   II. Series.

GV199.6.W47 1999   796.51
                             QBI98-1152

To Joy

Acknowledgements:

Kathleen Wheeler
Phyllis Carter
Jim Clinkscales
Mark Suchomel
Lynn's Photo
ColorType
Alison Thatcher
Tammy Parsons
Bookcrafters
Jim Waide
Alan Lachica

Plan for fun

Like any active pursuit outside the workplace, backpacking is supposed to be fun and challenging. Surviving horrible situations make for good stories, but it's the pleasure of accomplishment and the pure joy of being outdoors that we're concerned with here. **Planning and preparation are key.** With them your backpacking goals are reasonably attainable. Without them you'll be hating life. And you'll never go back.

Doug Werner

Just seven miles into a 45-mile hike.

Contents

Getting off outdoors.

Introduction:

Rewards

The ultimate anti-dote to modern living is the out-doors. Natural surroundings speak of beauty, eternity and true origins. There's an ageless order that sorts out the mundane and creates a primary perspective.

Simply put, it's a place to become recharged and refreshed. It's more than that, but it's difficult to describe very well because the spiritual refurbishment sounds like religion. And that misses the mark. For folks who allow themselves to know, the natural world is an enormously comforting place to be. Comforting to know how great it is and how small we are in it.

Roving about in a natural place yields a number of rewards: physical challenge, wondrous sights, breathing sweet and fresh air, sharing space with wild creatures. Moments you take back and cherish in your mind one thousand times. The profound satisfaction of self-reliant

behavior runs deep. Tiny triumphs feel Olympic. Like lighting a match in damp weather. Character is built and rebuilt in a place that demands every moment of your attention. And that you succeed.

Backpacker's Start-Up is an introduction to this roving about for modern people. Hiking and camping in the wild requires an attitude and a load of preparation. This book covers the essential gear, preparations, precautions and techniques required for dayhiking and short backpacking trips. Stuff is straight to the point and backed with insightful first hand experiences that beginners can relate to easily.

Getting started the right way:

Dayhikes

My wife and I dayhiked for years. Scores of hikes of various distances over different terrain in all kinds of weather. Before we ever considered backpacking, we were accustomed to the pounding in our joints and the utter weariness of occasionally hiking too long and far. We knew the importance of hiking with essential gear because we had suffered without a time or two.

Our hikes averaged around 10 miles, but there were times we covered up to 20 in a day. Three times we hiked from 5,000 feet to 10,000 feet (and back) covering more than 16 miles. With friends I hiked up and down Mt. Whitney (14,494 feet) in a day and that's a 22-mile journey.

Hiking in and out while the sun's up defines dayhiking. You need little beyond proper footwear, clothing and water to enjoy a complete escape into

Not another soul around.

nature. Your dayhiking experiences can be so fulfilling that you may never feel the need to camp. Once you've developed as a hiker, 10-, 15-, even 20-mile excursions are very doable in a day. You'll reach (and come back from!) those places that you once only dreamed of or saw on the nature channels.

If your ultimate goal is to pack it in for days on end, dayhiking is where you begin and develop.

The physical challenge

Dayhiking will get you used to the physical and mental requirements needed for tromping over miles of natural terrain. You'll use certain muscles to go up and different muscles to go down. You'll feel the pounding in hips, knees, ankles and feet. Although we all walk every

day, most don't do it in five-mile chunks over hill and dale. Like any new physical activity your body will complain the next day or two after a hike, but you will grow accustomed to the new exercise over time.

Trees, trees, trees!
Nature is so boring!

The right mind set

Hiking, of course, isn't like driving a car. It may take an hour to travel only two or three miles. For most modern people it's *Really Slowing Down*, this hiking business. Some become annoyed and bored with mere plodding and what seems to be an unchanging setting *(if you've seen one tree, you've seen them all!)*. The joy of hiking may take time to discover. It's not often a rush or a thrill. A hiker needs to

Typical daypack.

Fanny pack.

Absolutely,
always,
never forget.

develop patience as well as leg strength and stamina. *Patience for what?* I can almost hear certain readers exclaim. Well, that's for you to discover for yourself.

Daypack and essential gear

Carry what you need in a small daypack or fanny pack. Even with overkill, the loaded pack shouldn't weigh much more than a very manageable 10 pounds. Anything under 20 pounds can be comfortably supported by your shoulders. There are a number of simple, quality daypacks to choose from. There are models with hip belts as well. Consider using a fanny pack for light loads. This is a very small pack that simply buckles around the waist.

What to pack for a short, warm weather dayhike: Pullover, energy bar, map, poncho, water, tissue and Ziploc.

What you absolutely need is water. You'll also need protective clothing to keep warm and dry if it gets wet and cold. Bring a quart of water for every five miles of hiking or a water filter if you know you're hiking next to a water source. Pack rain gear and a pullover. Also pack fruit and energy bars for snacking, toilet paper and Ziploc bags to pack out the used toilet paper.

Further information about footgear, clothing, the outdoor toilet and safety are in those chapters so-named.

The Ten Essentials
You may want to consider "The Ten Essentials." First developed by the Mountaineers in the 1930s as a part of their climbing course, this is your basic kit for a worst-case scenario (getting lost and spending the

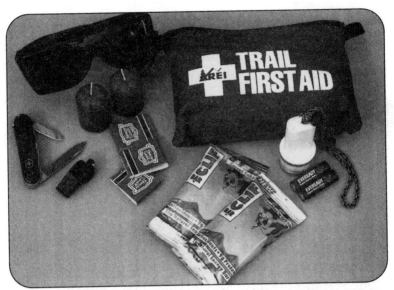

The so-called Ten Essentials include sunglasses, knife, candles (firestarters), matches, extra food, flashlight (with extra batteries), first aid kit, map and compass. Don't knock the senior's shades. They provide complete protection and fit over regular frames.

night). Some of this stuff may be overkill depending on where you're going and for how long.

1. Extra clothing
2. Sunglasses
3. First aid kit
4. Extra food
5. Flashlight/ batteries
6. Map
7. Compass
8. Matches
9. Firestarters
10. Knife

Dayhiking menu
Examples of things to pack and eat include sandwiches
of all sorts, cheese and crackers, dried fruit, granola and
energy bars. It's best to keep it simple and light, of
course. You can always load up before or after and not
even bother with a planned meal. Not so, however,
with water.

Building up to it
Start with short dayhikes over easy, well-marked terrain
with little altitude gain or loss. From five–eight miles
(two–three hours).

Increase distance and difficulty as you become accustomed to the exercise. You'll find it takes longer to
cover hilly or mountainous terrain. Up to 10 miles
(four–five hours).

Stay hydrated. Don't wait until you're
thirsty to drink. Always hike with water
(or near a water source from which you
can filter water).

Go for it when
you feel like it.
Try 12-15 miles
(five–six hours).

First hike
Plan to hike five
miles your first
time out.

Where?
Look at a good
map of your area.
In our country
there are innu-
merable natural

places set aside to enjoy a hike. It's one of the wonderful things about our culture. Despite the dire talk of a disappearing nature, parks have been set aside by cities, states and the United States federal government for many, many years. The resource section has more detailed answers to this question, but chances are a place to begin your hiking career is very near. You probably already know where it is.

You will need:
- Map
- Proper footwear
- Daypack
- Proper clothing including protection from potential cold or wet weather
- 1 quart of water for each person and/or a water filter
- 1 or 2 energy bars for each person
- Small roll of toilet paper
- Ziploc bag

Physical considerations and slogans
Your first five miles may seem like a lot. The last mile may seem endless (the last mile always will). To use a well-worn phrase, "No pain, no gain." To steal a well-known slogan, "Just Do It." Both are apt. But so is "Take it Easy." Perhaps "Stretch, Don't Break" is the more suitable cliché.

Attitude
You may love it right away or you may find it tedious. Hiking is not jumping with action. If your hike were a television or radio program, it would be full of "dead air." The value of hiking is measured and filled by the

quiet, steady pace. It may take some time to tune in. Give it (and yourself) a chance.

STORY: Crybaby

Some folks don't get it right away. It's not like the movies. There isn't a lot of immediate stimulation. A hike with friends was slightly marred because one person became frantic with the pace. Unused to the slow rhythms of a hike, she exclaimed after about a mile: *What are we doing! What's there to see! Look there's a tree! Turn the bend and there's another just like it! What's the use!* Angry and frustrated she clumped back to the cabin to watch television and drink wine. Oh well. At the time I was happy her head simply didn't explode.

Parting words

- Start with a few miles over flat or gently rolling terrain.
- Build up the miles and increase difficulty from hike to hike incrementally.
- Take stock of your efforts both physically and mentally (be patient).
- Take regular rest and water breaks.

Overnights

Backpacking

Our first backpacking trip was almost a bust. What saved us was our tolerance to certain discomforts and good preparation. We rented stove, tent and backpacks from REI and set out with a fair idea how to backpack with the stuff. It was a hot, hot summer afternoon with too many bugs. The packs were heavy and maladjusted. Swarming insects were so prevalent at our campsite we had to crawl into our tent by 6 p.m. It was a long, boring evening and a sleepless night punctuated with those awful where-am-I dreams.

But the morning was cool and pleasant and the hike back, over golden meadows, was quite nice. We took pride in being able to carry all the camping gear upon our backs and making everything work. It felt like an accomplishment and despite the drawbacks we looked forward to a greater challenge.

This is the great transition. Great because you must carry what you need for a night outdoors, and it's quite

It's a big, heavy pack. But it's something you can grow accustomed to.

considerable compared to dayhiking. Many hikers opt to remain dayhikers, and that's OK. I dayhiked for years before I tried backpacking. I saw those huge packs on backpackers and thought I'd never, ever do that. *How could that be any fun?*

Packing for short overnight trips is very similar to longer trips. After all, you'll need to bring tent, sleeping bag and pad, cooking gear, toilet kit, emergency essentials, food and clothing. The only difference is that you're carrying less food and clothing. It's still a big, heavy pack.

Getting used to it

Your first overnight should be light on distance. Hike in, say, two–four miles. Just enough to get acquainted with carrying 30–40 pounds. It takes getting used to! And problems might happen.

First of all, this is the first true test of the adjustment of your pack. Who knows, it may not be fitted quite right. After two miles the straps might be dissecting your shoulders. Or a strap could pop. Or it just feels like hell and you don't know why.

Even if the pack feels good (as it should!), your steps will be heavier. So this is also the first true test of your footwear. Shoes or boots may feel fine without a load, but may not support your feet properly with a full backpack. Your feet may flatten and swell with the load over time and start to burst the seams or even hit the end of your boots. It happens and it's miserable!

If pack and boots are OK, you'll only have to deal with the new physical effort of carrying a substantial load upon hips, back and shoulders — the pack driving into hip bones, the itch under shoulder straps and your back crying *Free Me!* Stepping up rocky grades is like doing weighted squats with one leg. Losing your footing is a serious strain on ankles. Falling with a sack on your back is ... well, you get the picture. Don't get me wrong. A pack can be worn safely and comfortably for miles and miles, but it takes a while to grow accustomed to it.

Have the time, patience and energy to make camp. Especially the first time!

Time to make camp
Besides learning to hike with a full pack, you'll need daylight as well as reserves of patience and energy to make camp for the first time. Although you've practiced putting up the tent and lighting the stove at home, how will it go when you really need your gear to cooperate? You're

actually going to sleep in the tent this time and cook over that fussy stove. Then there's clean-up, digging your first latrine, fumbling in the dark, dealing with bugs, preparing your sleeping pad and bag and so on. Making camp is one chore after another until you zip up and close your eyes.

It's supposed to be fun. Take plenty of rest and water breaks. Establish a comfortable pace and stick with it.

Your first backpacking trips should be trial runs. You're testing and breaking in equipment as well as yourself. There are a lot of parts and procedures involved in backpacking. Nothing very complicated or difficult, really — it just seems that way at first. It gets tricky only if you haven't planned and packed properly, or if you try to bite off too much at once.

Keep the distance short enough to safely endure (survive) the mishaps if they happen. If something really does go wrong, you're only a few miles from car and civilization.

22

Longer trips

After a successful overnight, there's no reason to be afraid of extended trips. Once you're comfortable with equipment, sure of your needs outdoors and satisfied with your hiking performance, then by all means go.

Increase distances and nights outside incrementally. Go five–six miles a day for two days, then three. If all goes well on shorter runs, go back further, climb higher and spend more nights on the trail. Allow yourself the option to go back if things don't work out.

Slip into outdoorsperson-mode carefully. Remember it's supposed to be fun. And like anything else, the more you hike and camp, the better you'll get at it.

First backpacking trip

Plan to hike two–four miles in, camp overnight and hike back out.

Where?

A local map may yield some answers, otherwise check out the resource section under **Finding Trails**.

You will need:

More than a few things. Read the rest of the book!

The physical challenge

It's not easy hiking with a 40-pound pack. It gets easier after you get going. Over time you can develop a tolerance, even a taste for it. But it's a real chore at first. Plan your distances carefully. It's better to feel that you could have done more after a hike than to feel beaten and exhausted.

Hiker's Hero: We met Jonathan at Rae Lakes in Kings Canyon, California. He hikes by himself in the Sierra back country each year from April until September (he works construction in the winter). His diet? Noodles and Snickers.

Attitude

Determine why you are backpacking on a given trip. Is it a pleasant escape from the day to day or is it a race against time and distance? The latter may become an ugly trial if you're not experienced, prepared or in tiptop physical condition.

It's wise to leave expectations at the trail head and take the hike one or two miles at a time. Take regular rest and water breaks — like every hour. Advance through your hike in a steady manner. Let the terrain, weather conditions and your body dictate the pace of your hike and the distance you cover. There is a proper pace for every hike. Furthermore, there is a proper pace for every portion of a hike. Get in sync with it.

STORY: Hiking heros

There's an outdoor culture that continues to astonish me. Every time I get back in there far enough I find someone else who's been so much further back for a lot longer. I was on a 45-mile trek and thinking I was some kind of Daniel Boone when I ran into three young men *loping* (yeah loping) through a 100-mile journey. As they sped by I noticed they were wearing sandals! Later on I meet some superman who ran my 45-mile trip in 12 hours carrying only a bottle of water and some power bars. That night I went on about how tough the day's hike had been to a fellow camper. He told me he was on his way to Canada from Mexico. So much for braggadocio. I'm just a wet noodle with this crowd.

Parting words

- Dayhike several hikes before you backpack.
- Hike in only a short distance at first. Maybe only a mile or two.
- Allow plenty of daylight to make camp.
- Increase distance and difficulty of hikes gradually.
- Monitor your effort and take frequent water, rest and assessment breaks.

The footgear pictured above tramped over the same 45 miles of rugged Sierra terrain. The boots worked very well yielding only one small hot spot. The sneakers caused giant bloody blisters that nearly crippled the hiker. In an attempt to relieve the pressure caused by expanding feet, slits were cut as indicated.

Footgear

Hurting feet are right up there with toothaches and earaches. When it happens nothing else matters but the cessation of the pain. It's overwhelming and incapacitating. I've had perfectly happy feet decide to grow an inch on a hike and painfully pound against the toes of the boots until my feet became so cramped I couldn't walk. I've witnessed the desperate effort of a friend to alter ill-fitting hiking shoes by chopping and slitting out the sides and toes. Still he suffered blisters that grew into ugly, flesh-eating wounds that took several days to heal.

Nothing is more important than your feet on a hike. **What you wear on them should fit comfortably each and every step of the way.** If you're hiking in inclement weather you'll need to wear footwear that keeps feet warm and dry.

Other than that, it's up to you. I'm not going to suggest you wear a certain type of boot with specific characteristics because I've seen experienced hikers wear different things very successfully. I've met top-flight outdoors people wearing sneakers, even sandals on their long, arduous treks.

Before you set out on longer hikes, test your footwear on short walks to make sure shoes (or whatever) are

The Vibram sole with a beefy lug for traction and protection from rocky trails.

well broken in. **If you're going to carry a pack, make sure you take test runs with that same pack (fully loaded).**

I wear boots that cover and support the ankles with a tough, pliable, water-resistant leather upper. I need to wear ankle-high boots to support my weak ankles. My ligaments in that area have long since stretched beyond repair due to numerous sprains. Every time I misstep, my ankles can break up to 90 degrees.

I also like thick durable soles (so I don't feel all the rocks and roots I clamber over) with a deep lug (tread) for traction.

I like my boots made of tough, strong materials so I won't stub my toes easily.

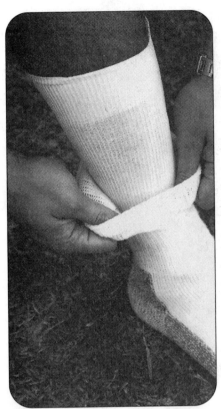

And I like to step lightly.

With these requirements I end up with a high ticket item. A pair of boots like that cost $140–200.

Socks
Do not wear cotton socks. They'll get wet with perspiration causing friction and blisters.

Wear synthetic liners made for hiking underneath wool or synthetic wool socks.

Wearing synthetic liners underneath synthetic wool socks helps keep feet dry.

The liners keep your feet dry by wicking the perspiration from feet to outer sock. There the moisture can begin to evaporate. One still needs to change liners and socks periodically during a hike to make sure feet remain dry. Make sure you bring at least two pair of each.

Blisters
The most common malady. Prevent them by insisting on good fitting boots, wearing liners and changing liners and socks to keep feet dry. Inexperienced feet

will get blisters anyway so keep initial forays short until feet toughen. Try moleskin or bandages on areas prone to blistering before you set out. Be aware of hot spots on your feet before blisters form and apply moleskin.

STORY: Daft

Ill-fitting boot stories are common and ugly. Most are born out of stupidity, haste or frugality. It's always the same: Ten miles into the hike and you wish you had taken your footwear seriously. Cramped and blistered feet are heinously painful and quite nearly debilitating. Fun no more, the trail becomes a trial.

My worst case involved steel-toed work boots. I thought since they performed so well in a warehouse that they'd be just the ticket on the trail. But the steel was ice cold in the mornings and eventually chewed into my toes. Often you can find folks to commiserate with — others who have suffered in the same way. But I stand alone. Never have I heard of anyone else daft enough to hike in steel-toed shoes.

Parting words
- Wear footwear that you know will be comfortable on the trail with a loaded pack.
- Keep your feet dry.

- Bandage hot spots immediately.
- Treat blisters immediately.

Labels to look for
Asolo
Garmont
Hi-Tec
M2
Merrell
Montrail
Raichle Gore-Tex
REI
Salomon
Tecnica
Vasque
Zamberlan

Mail order
REI 800-426-4840
www.rei.com
Campmor 800-226-7667
www.campmor.com

Price tags
Boots $45–200*
Liners $3
Socks $6

*Price ranges are approximate.

It's very important to try on new hiking boots with a fully loaded pack. Feet expand with added weight and exercise.

Clothing

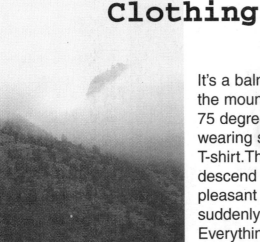

It's a balmy sunny day in the mountains. Maybe 75 degrees. You're wearing shorts and T-shirt. Then the clouds descend into your pleasant valley and it's suddenly 45 degrees. Everything turns moist. During the night the moisture freezes (it's gone down to 32 degrees!) leaving a thick frost on all your gear. Have you packed clothing to keep you comfortably warm and dry as summer becomes winter in less than an hour? It can happen that fast. It's bad enough when you're prepared. It's a crisis when you're not.

Wear and pack clothing that will keep you warm and dry in the worst-case scenario.

● The weather is a variable, especially in the mountains. **Prepare for the worst.**

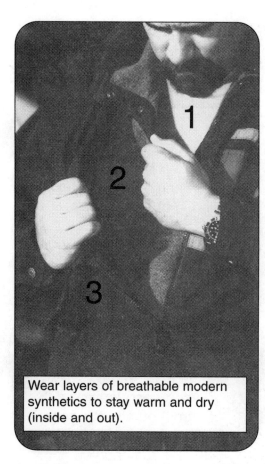

Wear layers of breathable modern synthetics to stay warm and dry (inside and out).

● **Dress in layers.** Makes it fast and easy to warm up or cool down.

● You are wise to **wear modern synthetic outdoor clothing that "breathes."**

Layering
This is the modern system that moves moisture away from the body. Of particular concern is the torso in colder temperatures.

1st layer: Next to the skin wear one of the high-tech, knit polyester materials. They wick (draw) sweat from skin to the outer layers of clothing where it can evaporate. **Never wear cotton T-shirts!** Cotton gets wet, stays wet and robs the body of body heat.

Middle layer(s): Wear layers of pile or fleece (more high-tech, polyester material). These fabrics are warm, nonabsorbent and breathe.

Third layer: The ideal is a breathable wind- and water-

proof shell or jacket. Such garments are made of fabric with pores smaller than water molecules (rain) but larger than water vapor molecules (body vapors). Thus, rain is repelled but vapors from the body pass through. Gore-Tex is the major brand.

The non-breathable waterproof shells are less expensive. Look for vents.

Special note
Goose down is a lighter and more compact insulator than synthetic fills, but loses its insulating capabilities when wet.

Shorts and pants
Wear durable shorts (a canvas/cotton mix is good) down to 40–50 degrees. As the air chills, cover legs with lightweight polyester, nylon, coated nylon or Gore-Tex pants. In very cold temperatures wear synthetic long johns under pants. **No cotton blue**

jeans. They are heavy, cold and slow to dry.

Warm weather
Shorts and T-shirts are OK. Shirts made of warm-weather synthetics are better since cotton stays wet from sweat.

Just in case: Take along a waterproof windbreaker or poncho, a synthetic (best) pullover for warmth and a hat with a brim.

In heat and intense sun, wear loose-fitting, light-colored, long-sleeve shirts and pants (dark colors absorb heat). Wear a light-colored, broad-brimmed hat to protect neck and face.

Rain gear
Breathable Gore-Tex or similar material are best (although breathability can be impaired by heat and sweat generated by uphill climbing and/or dirt). Non-breathable rainsuits (look for vents) or ponchos are much less expensive.

Hat
A bare head loses up to 25% of a hiker's body heat. Wear a warm synthetic or wool hat if it's cold.

Gloves

Waterproof and breathable gloves are best.

Sunglasses

Your eyes need protection from harmful ultraviolet rays which are intensified by higher altitudes and snow glare.

STORY: Lesson

Stay warm and dry! is not just some hiking book mantra. Coming down after a three-day trip in the Sierras, the weather suddenly turned. It was raining at 7,000 feet but we were within ten miles of our car by then and made it back with no problem. At the trailhead we heard it was snowing at the higher altitudes. We counted our blessings and drove home.

The next morning the newspaper reported the tragedy of a hiker who got hypothermia at 12,000 feet and never made it back. He was in the same park and died about the time we were getting wet at 7,000 feet. He was perhaps 8–10 miles away from us at the time. Like us, he thought the warm, sunny weather would hold for his entire trip. Although the article said he was an experienced outdoorsman, he apparently did not pack enough warm clothing. He got wet, his body grew cold and he became unable to walk. By the time rescuers got to him he was gone.

Parting words

- Wear modern, synthetic materials designed for the outdoors, especially in cold and wet weather.
- Wear and pack clothing that will keep you warm and dry in the worst-case scenario.

Labels to look for
Campmor
Camp-Tech
Columbia Sportswear
Duofold (underwear)
Fox River (socks and gloves)
Glenpile
Lowe Alpine
Marmot
Outdoor Products
Outdoor Research (hats and gloves)
Patagonia
Polartec
REI
Sierra Designs
Smartwool (socks)
Sportif USA
The North Face
Thorlo (socks)
Turtle Fur (hats)
Wickers (underwear)
Wigwam (socks)
Windstopper (hats and gloves)

Mail order
REI 800-426-4840 www.rei.com
Campmor 800-226-7667 www.campmor.com
Land's End www.landsend.com
LL Bean www.llbean.com

Price tags

Underwear, shirt	$16–45*
Underwear, pants	$16–37
Insulating layer, pullover	$30–70
Insulating layer, pants	$30–98
Outer shell, parka	$80–389
Outer shell, pants	$40–295
Shorts	$17–40
Pants	$27–72
Rain gear, jacket	$29–59
Rain gear, pants	$15–39
Rain gear, poncho	$5
Hat	$10–35
Gloves	$12–50
Sunglasses	$16–80

*Price ranges are approximate.

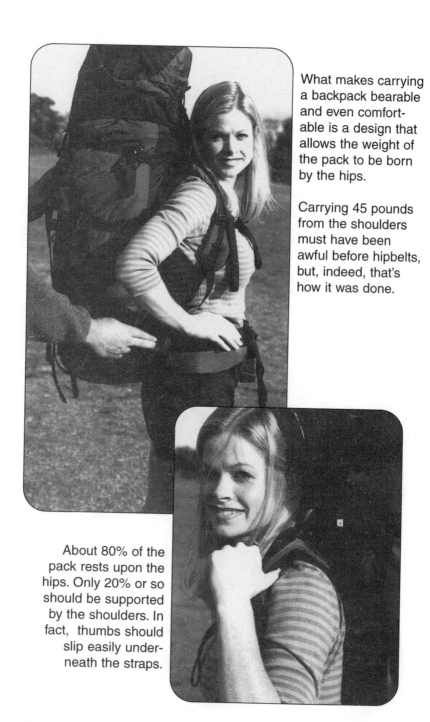

What makes carrying a backpack bearable and even comfortable is a design that allows the weight of the pack to be born by the hips.

Carrying 45 pounds from the shoulders must have been awful before hipbelts, but, indeed, that's how it was done.

About 80% of the pack rests upon the hips. Only 20% or so should be supported by the shoulders. In fact, thumbs should slip easily underneath the straps.

Backpacks

The first thing I noticed upon putting on a good fitting backpack was how comfortable it felt. As a dayhiker I was used to straps cutting into my shoulders. Feeling the weight on my hips was a wonderful new dimension. That was the moment I began to think that maybe this backpacking business wasn't such a mule-ish, masochistic endeavor after all.

Backpacks have a rigid supporting frame. This enables a hiker to carry more than with a typical daypack which usually dangles from shoulder straps. **The frame distributes the weight off the shoulders to the hips.** A hipbelt is necessary.

There are two kinds of backpack frames: Alan's **external frame** (left) has a rigid metal or plastic support on which the bag hangs. Alison's **internal frame** has metal stays constructed inside the pack.

The external frame supports the pack away from the body. This allows the air to evaporate the sweat from your back. Since it rigidly holds the load away from your body, it doesn't move precisely with your motion. It can sway and throw you off balance. If you hike on trails this is not a problem. But for off-trail, rock scrambling or stream crossings it can be.

Compared to the internal frame the external frame costs less, is easy to fit and easy to load.

The internal frame fits close to the body. Originally designed to work off-trail in demanding terrain, this pack moves with a hiker's motion and many hikers like that. Internals are somewhat complicated and can be more difficult to fit. Without a support to hold the pack open, it is more difficult to pack. Internals are more expensive than comparable

external-frame packs.

If you're going to climb, thrash and wade off-trail, the internal frame is your pack.

Fitting

Try on both styles with a load. **Most of the weight should settle on the hips.** In fact, your

Alison has no problem negotiating a narrow trail with her slimmer internal-frame pack.

shoulder straps should carry only about 20% of the weight. Fingers should slip easily underneath. If they cut into your shoulders, something's wrong. There is adjusting to do! The pack must fit your torso length (base of neck to top of hip) as well as your waist and hips. Look for adjustable models in

Alan gets hung up on the same path with his wider external frame.

The external-frame pack boasts a framed, top-loading mouth that makes packing easy.

your size (yes, many pack models come in sizes) and to fit your specific body type. There are packs specifically designed for women as well as men.

A good fit feels good on your back. Expect the 40 pounds or so to settle you down a bit, but comfortably. You may be amazed at just how easily your hips support a fully loaded pack. I certainly was.

Stick with the major brands (see "labels" at end of chapter) to ensure quality. **Insist on knowledgeable help.** You will need it to adjust the pack to your body.

Size

Pack size is measured in cubic inches. External frames of 4,000 to 5,000 cubes will carry a week's worth of gear and grub. Internal frames of 4,500 to 6,000 cubes will do the same. They are larger because the sleeping bag is packed inside the pack. The bag is lashed outside external-frame packs.

Daypacks

Anything under 20 pounds can be comfortably supported by your shoulders. There are a number of simple, quality daypacks to choose from. There are

models with hipbelts as well. Consider using a fanny pack for light loads.

STORY: It's your back

Packing too much is apparently a common practice. I've heard of packs weighing 60 pounds or more and I don't understand that at all. I lug about 45 pounds or so and that's it. I'll eat the bark off trees before I carry any more than that. We met a young lady once who was out by herself with a pack that must have weighed 75 pounds. She had food packaged in the same glass jars they came in as well as a teddy bear to snuggle with at night (not that teddies are heavy, but they can be bulky hence space consuming). On the same trip we heard about a fellow who was so exhausted from his burden that he discarded brand-new gear to lighten his load. In contrast, we encountered someone later on who didn't have 25 pounds on his back. He thought himself a wuss for carrying that much.

What should *you* carry? Exactly what *you need*, and you won't know that (exactly) until you've done it a few times. But trust me, you can leave teddy at home.

Parting words

- Purchase or rent a name brand pack that fits well when fully loaded.
- Make sure your backpack rests on your hips comfortably. Your shoulders carry maybe 20% of the weight. The straps should not dig.

Labels to look for
External frame
Camp Trails
Dana Design
JanSport
K2
Kelty
REI

Internal frame
Arc'Teryx
Camp Trails
Eagle Creek
Gregory
Kelty
Lowe
Mountainsmith
REI
The North Face

Mail order
REI 800-426-4840 www.rei.com
Campmor 800-226-7667 www.campmor.com

Price tags

External frame	$120–190*
Internal frame	$175–300
Daypacks	$30–55

Renting

External frame	$10–20 first day. $5–10 each additional day. $50 deposit.
Internal frame	$15–25 first day. $5–10 each additional day. $50 deposit.

*Price ranges are approximate.

It looks like a lot but if the pack fits, 45 pounds will not be a problem for this hiker.

47

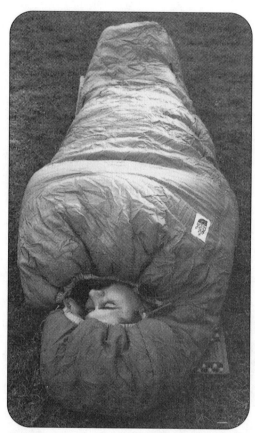

Achieving a comfortable night's sleep is of supreme importance. Without it your hike will become an endurance test.

Chapter Five:

Sleeping bags & pads

When I was kid sleeping bags were like big thick
blankets with a zipper around the perimeter. They still
make them like that but they're not for backpacking.
What you need is a tapered, lightweight mummy bag
that will seal you from the cold.

**Buy a mummy bag. It's the standard for back-
packing.** They are narrow, light and conserve body
heat. It has a hood that envelopes the head and traps
warm air.

Bags come with a temperature rating. That's the temperature you'll begin to feel cold. **Get 20 degrees or
less for most warm-weather camping.**

**Choose between goose down or synthetic fiber
fill.**

PROS & CONS
Down
● Lighter.
● More compact.
● More durable.
● More comfy over a wide range of temperatures
  because down breathes better than synthetic.
● May cause allergic reactions.
● Initially more expensive (but lasts longer).

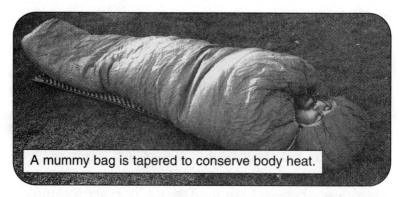

A mummy bag is tapered to conserve body heat.

- Requires more care (must wash with special soaps). **Takes a long time to dry. Loses loft and warmth when wet.** (Loft is a bag's ability to fluff up, trap air and insulate.)

Synthetic
- **Drys more quickly. Retains loft when wet and up to 85% of a sleeper's body heat.**
- Stuffing over time breaks down loft.

More bag bullets
- An ideal bag weight for backpacking is three pounds or less.
- Use a bag liner to add warmth (up to 20 degrees) and to keep the inside of your sleeping bag cleaner.
- Wear dry clothes and a cap to extend the temperature range of your bag.
- Look for an insulating strip behind the zipper and a well-shaped mummy hood and drawstring.
- You may need to buy a larger stuff sack since you may not be able to restuff your bag into the manufacturer's original stuff sack.
- Don't store your bag in the stuff sack. This compresses the fibers, reduces the loft and damages your

bag's insulating capability. Hang or gently fold after the hike.

Peeing in your bag

I suppose one of the major hassles in camping has to be getting out and back into a sleeping bag during the night because you must take a leak. Here's a hint for the guys: Snuggle up with a plastic bottle. Those wide mouth juice containers work pretty well. Make sure the cap screws down tight.

STORY: Less

On a biking/camping trip through Catalina Island, I slept on a discarded shower curtain under a simple blanket. Each night before I turned in I gathered a heap of leaves and pine needles to sleep on. It was amusing to the more expansively equipped on the trip — those with mummy bags, specially designed sleeping pads and tents (even I had to admit it was a bit eccentric) — but I slept great for less (less bulk, less weight, less hassle, less expense).

On the trail simply stuff your bag (without rolling it up) into its sack. However, after the hike unstuff it and let it hang in order to preserve loft.

Only two things had me concerned — wart hogs and the buffalo that roamed through our camp at night. Without a tent I was afraid of being routed or stepped on. Neither happened, although a group of buffalo did gather within a few feet to munch on a nearby bush sometime in the wee hours. I simply sat up and kept an eye on them until they left. (They are actually rather docile creatures, nothing like the ferocious beasts in the movies. A loud yell would have sent them scampering.)

My simple sleeping arrangement worked because the weather was warm and dry, there were no crawling bugs in my leaf mattress or flying insects biting and swarming around my head. Sometimes being outside isn't all that different from being inside (except for the buffalo!). On this particular trip, my Spartan preparations turned out to be the perfect solution for sleep.

Parting Words
● Buy a name brand mummy bag with a temperature rating of 20 degrees or less.

Sleeping Pads

Everything's perfect. Weather, plans, preparations, your physical and mental well-being. You've hiked 10 miles, made camp, prepared a decent meal and it's time to turn in. You bundle up in bag and tent and soon you're sawing Zs. Around 2 a.m. you wake on the hard ground. The sleeping pad has lost air. Sleep after that is intermittent and pocked with wicked dreams. Without a repair kit you can forget about enjoying the rest of your hike. You'll be counting the days to get back home to a good mattress and a full night's rest.

Closed-cell foam pad

You cannot sleep directly on the ground in your bag. You'll lose heat to the cold ground. Forget about comfort and a good night's sleep.

Backpackers opt for self-inflating foam mattresses or closed-cell foam pads.
The former is constructed of spongy, open-cell foam encased in a nylon shell. Closed-cell pads are made of a dense foam filled with enclosed air cells. **Do not use air mattresses. They will puncture and become useless.**

PROS & CONS
Self-inflating foam mattresses
- **Excellent insulation.**
- Most comfortable.
- Somewhat less bulky than closed-cell pads.
- Relatively heavy.
- More expensive.
- Can puncture, must carry a repair kit.

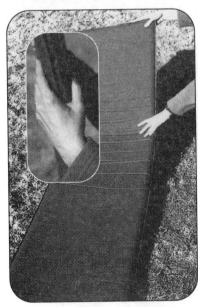

Self-inflating foam mattress

Closed-cell foam pad

- Good insulation.
- Little cushion.
- Light.
- Inexpensive.
- Indestructible.
- Use as sitting pad in camp.

Pillow

Use stuff sack or fleece pullover filled with clothing.

Parting words

- Buy a closed-cell pad or a self-inflating foam mattress with a repair kit.
- Never use a plain air mattress (the kind kids use in pools).

Labels to look for

Sleeping bags

Campmor
Coleman
Kelty
Marmot
REI
Sierra Designs
Slumberjack
The North Face

Sleeping pads

Cascade Designs
Therm-A-Rest
Slumberjack

The self-inflating foam mat can be converted into a comfortable camp chair. The closed-cell pad (pictured at top) is easily folded to make a sitting pad.

Mail order
REI 800-426-4840 www.rei.com

Campmor 800-226-7667 www.campmor.com

Price tags

Down mummy sleeping bag	$170–440*
Synthetic mummy sleeping bag	$120–305
Closed-cell sleeping pad	$12–25
Self-inflating mattress	$45–105
Bag liners	$29–107

Renting

Sleeping bag $10–30 first day.
$6–12 each additional day.
$50 deposit.

Sleeping pads $5–17 first day.
$1–6 each additional day.
$50 deposit.

*Price ranges are approximate.

Never use an air mattress. They're as cheap and useless as they look.

It's liberating to have all you need on your back. It appeals to lofty values lurking in us all: freedom, rugged individualism and self-reliance.

Art of packing

Spend the time to get what you need and to organize it in a pack. Spend a lot of time doing that! Pack at home so that when you reach the trailhead you simply put on the pack and take off. As you go on trip after trip the packing becomes easy and second nature. However, the first time can be fraught with indecision and frivolity.

Your life is in your pack. **It's your home.** Every time you break camp it's like leaving town for good. Every time you make camp it's like moving into a new house.

It's important to be well organized. Know where everything is. Use stuff sacks and label them. Pack items that go together in the same sack or pocket. Be consistent as you pack and unpack.

Weight of pack
It is written that an average man can carry 1/3 of his weight, a women 1/4. However, the ideal for back-packing is more like 1/5 of body weight.

Prepack
The first time you do this is the most time-consuming. If you're careful about packing and repacking, preparing for trips gets progressively easier.

Step One: Get all your stuff together ...

It helps to think *Combat Mission!* Or *Survival!* My wife just calls me *Anal!* The point is this: **Sloppy Does Not Work.** In order to have a fun, safe time you need to be a Class A Packer. No less.

Lay all your stuff out

● Repackage food items originally purchased in heavy, glass or leaky containers. Use plastic tubes available in outdoor stores and Ziplock bags. Organize the food in one or two sacks and further organize by day and meal if the menu is complex (which it should not be!).

● Like the food items, put kitchen items in a special sack, tent items in their own sack and so on. It helps to label each sack with its contents.

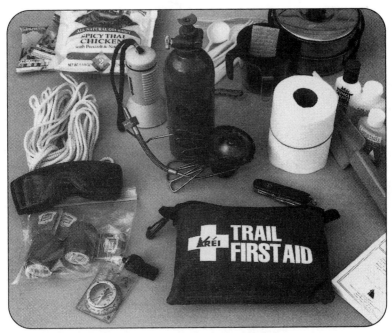

Step Two: Categorize and organize into piles ...

● Pack tent stakes in a separate bag within the tent bag so they can't puncture tent or anything else.

● Put clothing in a durable plastic bag or stuff sack to keep it dry.

● Look for ways to conserve space and to cut weight. Your ability to do that grows each trip you take. Once you've been out there, you will know what you need and when you need it.

Packing
● Keep items you need during the day handy:
Map! Water! Also snacks, pullover, poncho, moleskin, first-aid kit and fishing gear.

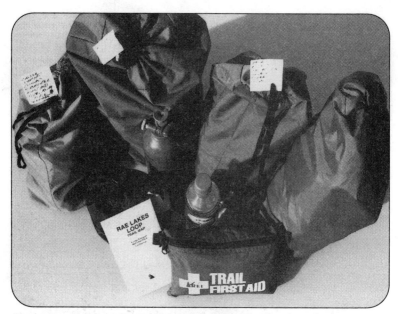

Step Three: Sack each organized pile ...

- Actually, a well-packed pack should provide easy access to everything (you bet!).
- Pack fuel separately from food (and everything else).
- Pad sharp-edged items.
- Distribute and balance your load carefully.

External frame packing
An external-frame pack is easier to load because of its open-mouth design.

Men
Load heavier gear on top, close to the back. This places weight up and over hips and feet. Example: Pack clothing at the bottom and food on top. Upper pockets hold water, fuel and snacks.

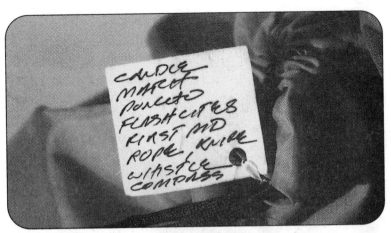

Step Four: Label each sack ...

Step Five:
Pack your sacks.
Create a symmetrical
and balanced load.

Women

Some women may
want heavier
items packed
lower since the
female center of
gravity is lower
(around the hips)
than the male
(around the
diaphragm).

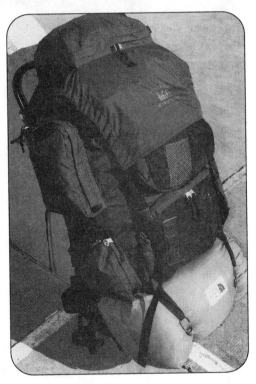

Lash your sleeping
bag to the bottom
(after packing pack) with small bungies or rope.

It's a load! Let a friend help.

Internal frame packing

The internal frame depends on the gear inside to keep its shape. There's no supporting frame or mouth. The sleeping bag always fits inside the pack on the bottom.

For off-trail hiking, pack heavier items lower and close to the back. Otherwise pack like an external. Again, women may want to pack heavier stuff lower.

Putting the backpack on

For best result: Use a raised, waist-high platform (rock, log, table) or get help from a friend.

Swing method

1. Plant your feet and flex your knees in a balanced, athletic position.
2. Grasp the shoulder straps.
3. Swing the pack onto your upper thigh or hip.
4. Slip an arm into the strap on that side.
5. Swing the pack to the other side and slip the other arm into the remaining strap.

Swing method: Alan makes it look easy. Better to use a raised platform or have a friend help at first.

Packing for dayhikes

Most important
Bring a quart of water for every five miles or so (each quart weighs two pounds). Or use a filter if you're hiking near a water source.

What we pack
We carry plenty of water and depending on the time of year, proper emergency apparel (pullovers for warmth, poncho for rain). We also pack fruit and nutrition bars for snacking, toilet paper and Ziplock bags to pack out the used TP.

A properly packed and adjusted pack looks good and feels good.

STORY: Whacky Packy?
Am I really such a Felix? On the last two backpacking trips, I packed the *other* person's pack as well as my own. I think I've reached a new level, but I don't know it by it's medical name. Hey, at least I know where everything is.

Parting Words
- Pack like items together in stuff sacks and label contents.
- Always pack and repack everything in the same sack in the same spot in your pack.

Tents

One of the nicer things about our high-tech age is the advent of modern tent design. I grew up in the age of stinky canvas pup tents that were nearly impossible to set up correctly. Stakes, guy lines, knots and wayward poles pushed and pulled in opposite directions. One side was always droopy and the tent never met the ground properly. Pup tents had no floors, no protection from bugs and they weighed a ton. If you faced any real weather, there was no guarantee that you'd stay warm and dry because the elements could swoosh in through the flaps or underneath the walls.

The modern tent can be buttoned up tight. There is a floor and all openings are sealed with zippers. Treated canvas is long gone and replaced with light, synthetic materials that let the tent breathe. They are a snap to erect and take down. Some don't even need stakes. With a properly fit rain fly you are warm and dry inside.

Two campers fit in this dome tent. Note the waterproof floor that extends up the walls. It's erect in two minutes.

You can do without, but ...

Modern tents are reliable, easy to use, eliminate the possibility of getting wet, cut wind, hold in body heat (up to 20 degrees warmer than outside), keep out insects and provide privacy.

Buy "three season"

Tents are categorized by "seasons." One- or two-season tents are designed for mild days and nights. A three-season tent can handle more difficult weather and is recommended. Four-season tents are built for serious outdoor conditions that the start-up camper will not be facing soon.

Tight fit

Tents are rated according to the number of people they hold (one, two, four, etc.). The number is based on a tight fit. If you plan to bring gear into the tent, make sure it'll fit.

A rain fly provides a waterproof layer over non-waterproof tent walls. The layering system allows the vapors from breathing campers to escape instead of condensing into drops of moisture inside the tent.

Rain flies should cover
past waterproof sidewalls.

Look for pockets and
loops to stash stuff.

Vestibules protect gear and even
provide a place to cook.

Look for

- Waterproof floors that come up several inches to line the lower walls of the tent.
- Interior features such as pockets and loops.
- A rain fly that covers the entire tent.

Tent types

A–Frame: Traditional. Sheds rain and wind well.
Dome: Provides the most interior space (as shown here).
Hoop or Tunnel: The lightest and most compact.

All tents come with poles and stakes. Many come with guy lines, seam sealer and a pole repair sleeve. New tents and accessories are neatly packed in compact stuff sacks.

Available in some tent types

Vestibule: An extra sheltered space for cooking, eating or storing gear.
Freestanding: The capability to be self-supporting without stakes (except in high wind).

Corded poles
snap into place ...

How hard is it to put up?
There are clip, sleeve and grommet systems. Count the number of connecting points between tent and tent poles. Count the number of stakes. The fewer the better.

A good test
Ask your salesperson to put up his favorite tent in five minutes or less.

... slide through
sleeves ...

Tent fabric
Most tents are made of strong, lightweight nylon taffeta or ripstop nylon. Floors and flies are coated with polyurethane or a moisture-repellent substance to prevent moisture from passing from the ground into tent.

Tent poles
Poles are shock-corded fiberglass or aluminum. They are threaded in segments which simply snap into place. They fold neatly into compact bundles.

Fiberglass poles are less expensive and more flexible than aluminum. They provide a better packing size. Fiberglass can be affected by weather. Aluminum is more durable.

... and are
secured at each
corner. It's up!
Note groundcover.

Workmanship
Look for: Lap-felled seams (like Levis)

that have four layers of interlocking fabric and double stitching. On uncoated nylon tents check for taped seams. Make sure stress points are reinforced with extra stitching or bar tacking.

Color (if you care)
When you're inside your tent:
Pale blue or green are appealing in bright sun. May be depressing in overcast weather. Orange and yellow are cheery in foul weather. The trend is toward gray, white and tan. Very bright or neon colors are for extreme camping.

Modern tent physics
A well-designed tent deals with moisture rising from inside as well as outside precipitation. A camper's breath and skin gives off water vapor that can condense and form drops on the walls of a tent. Today's tents have a non-waterproof wall and a separate, waterproof rain fly. The fly covers the tent leaving a space

between the layers. Vapors penetrate the tent wall and exit underneath the fly.

Pointers
● Use a waterproof ground cloth underneath the tent to protect the life of the built-in floor. It should not protrude beyond your tent's edges. Rain will puddle upon the protrusion and run underneath.

- Never bring in food since critters, bears especially, know no bounds.
- Use extra tarp roof for heavy rain.
- If it hasn't been done at the factory, seal seams with a waterproof seam sealer (needle holes may allow water into tent).
- Have a patch kit handy.
- Dig a moat around tent in heavy rain.

An option
A bivy bag is just big enough to fit you and your sleeping bag. It's the lightest, most compact shelter there is. It provides a waterproof barrier as well as warmth around your bag.

Before you pack up, lift the erect tent overhead to shake out any debris.

Picking a tent site
Look for a flat area or slight slope. Sleep with heads uphill. Find a sunny spot if it's cold. Beware of dead branches overhead.

After the hike
Wash and dry your tent thoroughly after trips. A good washing solution: five gallons water, eight ounces lemon juice, one tablespoon bleach.

STORY: Of old tents
Thirty years ago I took a trek across the country and spent a night in a trailer park in Vernal, Utah. As I was trying to set up

my old-fashioned pup tent about 15 very enthusiastic children came by to check me out. I immediately saw the opportunity and put them to work putting up my vintage WWII shelter. I hated erecting the thing with all its stakes, poles and guy lines. It took forever and it never seemed to look right when it was finally up. You have to wonder how our forefathers had time to win the Big One after pitching pup tents all afternoon.

The kids loved it though and they happily made a swarming effort until their mothers called them for supper. Of course, the tent was slanted and sloppy (as if I'd done the job myself) but it sufficed. The next morning one of those moms (together with a dad) asked me over for breakfast. I guess they were thrilled I let their little boy help me with the tent.

I don't know why this story has stayed on my mind for nearly 30 years. I don't know why I'm putting it here. Maybe it's because the event wouldn't happen these days. Tents are so easy to deal with now. Today you'd have a tent up before the kids even knew you were there. Maybe I remember because of the 15 helpful, happy faces and a generous family in the middle of nowhere. That smelly, problematic old tent brought me a little fellowship along a lonely stretch of road.

Parting words
- Buy or rent a modern,* easily erected, name brand, freestanding tent.

*Modern means lightweight, constructed with durable synthetic materials, complete with collapsible poles, a built-in floor and a good fitting rain fly. Freestanding means you don't need to use stakes (unless there's wind).

Labels to look for
Eureka!
Kelty
Marmot
REI
Sierra Designs
The North Face

Mail order
REI 800-426-4840 www.rei.com
Campmor 800-226-7667 www.campmor.com

Price tags
Two-person tent	$89–275*
Bivy	$150–275

Renting
Two-person tent	$15–25 first day
	$5–10 each additional day
	$50 deposit

*Price ranges are approximate.

Chapter Eight:

Water treatment

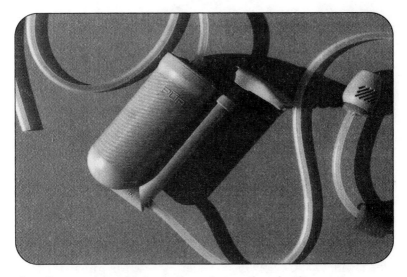

Another somewhat modern invention is the water filter. Stick one tube in the water, the other in a bottle and pump. With little effort you have safe water. No boiling or chemicals. Unless you're camping in the desert you don't have to lug water anymore.

Hikers can no longer safely drink directly from the clear, blue waters. The biggest hazard is giardia. A close second is cryptosporidium.

Giardia, #1 bad protozoan

Giardiasis a serious gastrointestinal disease (severe diarrhea, bloating, weakness) caused by the waterborne

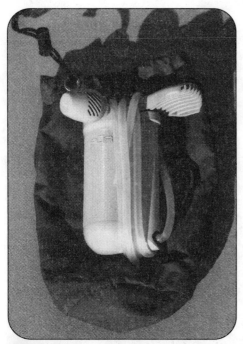

Water filters are small, light and compact. All you need is a natural source of water. At two pounds per quart, you don't want to know how much water you'd need to lug over a four-day hike without one of these things.

protozoan giardia lamblia. Any mammal can become infected and excrete live giardia in its feces. It gets into even the remotest sources of water. Giardia survives in snow and cold water as a cyst and is resistant to usual chemical treatments. Symptoms appear 6–15 days after exposure. It's debilitating and difficult to treat.

Water must be boiled or filtered down to two microns. Iodine treatment works but only with time and effort.

Cryptosporidium, #2 bad protozoan
Another bad bug! Chemicals don't work. Boil or filter way down to .4 microns.

Bacteria
Examples are cholera and salmonella. Boiling, iodine treatment and filtering works.

Viruses

Includes hepatitis A and B. Boil, use iodine treatment or a water purifier.

In order to avoid these awful diseases assume all open sources of water are contaminated.

Boiling

Boil drinking water for three–five minutes. (But this uses up precious fuel. And who wants to drink hot water?)

Water filters

Water filters are made that strain out giardia, cryptosporidium and bacteria.

Water filters are aces! You can pump up a bottle of drinkable water in no time. They're light and maintenance is a snap. For most hiking experiences, it's the way to go. No question.

Water purifiers

Water purifiers eliminate the tiniest bad guys: viruses. Most incorporate iodine treatment.

Iodine

It does not work against cryptosporidium. It works against bacteria and viruses.

Iodine is difficult to use properly against giardia. Use it as a back-up if you're not boiling or filtering. Bring water temperature to 70 degrees so that cysts will open and protozoans will be vulnerable to poison. (But who wants to do this?)

The problems with iodine treatment include chemical taste (unless filtered out with carbon) and prolonged treatment time if used in cold or murky water.

Consider iodine a good, inexpensive back-up system for all except the cryptosporidium protozoan.

It's heavy!
Water weighs two pounds per quart. A very good reason to buy a water filter and plan hikes around water sources!

Water rules
General rule: Drink one to two quarts of water per day.
Better rule: Drink water at regular intervals.
The rule: Never get thirsty!

STORY: Small wonder
The joy of backpacking is built upon small wonders and nuggets of appreciation. For example, I get a real charge out of getting a stove to work with one match. Finding something in my pack when I need it is always a shining moment.

The first time I used a water filter ranks as high as any of these small pleasures. The Kings River is a gorgeous Sierra stream that cascades over miles of rocky canyon. It's crystal clear but you cannot drink directly from it because of the giardia bug. However, if armed with a filter you can fill a bottle in a minute and wet your thirst without a qualm.

I remember holding the bottle up to the light to see how pure the water was. Not a spec! It was cold and delicious. Wonder gizmo meets nature on a higher plane. There is hope for a technological age.

Parting words
● Buy a name brand water filter capable of filtering bacteria (smallest of the typical bad "bugs").

Labels to look for
Katadyn
MSR
PUR
SweetWater

Mail order
REI 800-426-4840 www.rei.com
Campmor 800-226-7667 www.campmor.com

Price tags
Water Filters	$35–275*
Water Purifiers	$70–130

*Price ranges are approximate.

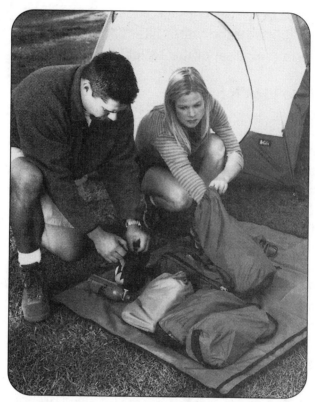

Whether you're coming or going, if you keep yourself organized the "work" part of camping gets
done faster and more efficiently. It starts with how
well you pack your pack. If you organize gear
properly there's a place for everything and everything's in its place. Lay it out and make your camp.
When it's time to leave repack carefully and put
gear back where it was. Simple.

Chapter Nine:

Making & breaking camp

The idea is to get the work part of camping done and over with as quickly and efficiently as possible.

Ignore those in your party who are muttering *Anal retentive! Control freak!* Give yourself time in the light and warmth of day to fumble around with everything. Setting up camp should take less than an hour (max!) but on your first trips allow for a learning curve.

Find a flat spot at least 100 feet from the stream or lake. A little slope is OK.

Spread a ground cover (which should be packed on top) **and lay out your stuff.** This way you can see what's what. There's the tent sack, there's the kitchen sack, there's the food sack, there's the flashlight, there's the garbage sack, and so on.

Set up sleeping quarters
Remove sticks and stones. Set up the tent so that your head is uphill. Since you've practiced putting up your tent at home, putting it up out here is a snap (really!).

Prepare and arrange your sleeping pads and bags. Place a flashlight in a handy spot. Zip it up.

Set up your kitchen

Find a flat place to set up your stove. An elevated flat spot on a rock is more convenient than squatting on the ground to cook. Make sure it's steady. Arrange utensils and food around the stove so that when cooking and eating commence there's no hide and seek. *(OK, the water's boiling. Hey, where's the food?)*

Set up your sanitation system

Identify and establish one trash bag.

Now get wood for your campfire

After establishing shelter and food stations, then go out looking for wood on the ground for campfires if permitted. Look for twigs (pencil thickness and smaller), smaller sticks up to an inch in diameter and thicker ones up to three inches. Be sure they are hard and dry. For directions on building a fire, see the "Stoves" chapter.

Cook, eat and drink

See the "Eating" chapter.

Clean up and pack up your garbage and strong smelling stuff and make it critter-proof. Look under "Bears" in the "Safety and Well-Being Chapter."

Pack for the night

Pack up and protect everything that you don't want wet from dew or nasty weather. Organize stuff so when you get up, clothes are handy, if it rains, rain gear is handy, if a bear shows up, your whistle is handy ...

Backpacking is an efficiency game. It involves a handful of simple systems that will deliver time and time again if you adhere to basic procedures and take care of your gear. That spacious tent folds down and fits into a small sack – tent, poles, stakes, repair kit, rain fly ... everything. Amazing.

Turning in

- Have flashlight and shoes ready for midnight pee excursions.
- Have tomorrow's clothing ready.
- Have your rain fly ready.
- Take off sweaty, dirty clothes.
- Sleep in clean and dry clothing.

Sleeping

Backpacking will be among the busiest activities, mentally and physically, that you'll ever do. You're either packing, unpacking, making preparations or hiking. Even when you're resting on the trail, you're mentally reviewing everything from the weather to the water supply. Sleeping is the only time you are not fussing with something. Enjoy it.

Try not to go to bed too early. Night falls fast, especially in the mountains and valleys. Seven p.m. can feel like 9 p.m. Keep yourself occupied with conversation, games or more interesting pursuits until well into the evening to prevent premature waking.

Breaking camp

After morning rituals (200 feet from the water), cooking, eating and utensil cleaning (50 feet from the water), it's time to put it all back in sacks and packs.

- Pack sleeping bags and pads in their sacks.
- Take down, roll up and pack your tent in its sack.
- Break down and pack up your kitchen in its sack.
- Put out the campfire. Spread the coals and douse with water until cool to the touch. Pack out those packaging items that didn't burn (like cans!).

- Neatly stack your wood leftovers.
- Walk through your site and pick up.
- Pack trash in the garbage bag and tie it off.
- Repack all the sacks back into your pack.
- Before you leave make sure the site is as appealing as you would like it to be for yourself.

It sounds like boot camp but ...

It helps to establish a routine with making and breaking camp. It makes for efficiency in time and effort. The better you get at this the more time you have to fish, frolic, loaf or contemplate the wonder of your navel or nature in general.

STORY: Gem

Backpacking trips are not 100% nirvana. You carry a load, the weather may be a problem, for whatever reason you may not sleep well, gear might not cooperate and someone always gets a blister. Of course, there's plenty of fun to be had at the time, but I think backpacking trips are deeply pleasurable and therapeutic for those moments you bring back with you. Memory gems that keep you going in front of a glowing screen or behind a farting bus.

My favorite memory is of an early evening next to the muffled roar of a mountain river. I was about to throw my line into the water when I looked back at our camp. We had just erected the tent next to a granite wall and in front of that I had started a wood fire that was burning down to a glowing bed of cooking coals. Kathleen was busy laying out a kitchen when she glanced up to wave and smile. Everything was lit the way a September's setting sun can light things — rich, warm, colorful — the moment before it extinguishes itself. The fire was reflected by the surrounding granite and our white dome tent. Purple shadows slowly framed the entire picture.

Transfixed, I felt like I had walked into a Remington painting, or a Jeep advertisement — the kind where they show a shiny new vehicle alongside a luminous tent next to a pretty lake. The headline says something about getting away from it all. Our camp was perfect. The scene was perfect. The memory is perfect and will remain one of those gems that remind me of what can be real (and available to return to) forever.

Parting words
- Develop a procedure. Unpack, create a sleeping station, create a kitchen station and so on.
- Don't listen to anybody who complains about your management style.

Eating

Dining can be overrated on the trail. If you're really exerting yourself and enjoying the outdoors, most anything will taste wonderful. Keep it simple, nutritious and filling. Gourmet, no.

Keep it simple

I think knowing a little something about nutrition is a good thing. It gives you a handle on what you need to eat. And preparing tasty meals in the woods is a wonderful thought. But somehow it's easy to go overboard with backpacking menus. You think you must pack this in order to eat that and you need all the other to prepare it properly.

Nuts to that.

You don't need to cook at all. A proper menu of water, energy bars, fruit and trail mix will keep you going. Think about it: No cooking, no clean up and less to carry on your back.

What the body needs is simple. It needs water more than anything else. In fact, you can survive without food for at least a week (not that I'm suggesting you try that), but water you must have on a regular basis or the body breaks down.

Don't get me wrong. I think eating is a real highlight when I'm hungry. Especially after grinding out ten miles with a 45-pound pack. But what keeps me going and what keeps me happy is not all that difficult to pack and prepare. And I don't think I'm alone on this one. Most any-thing you eat out there is going to taste great because you have a healthy hunger and, after all, you're outdoors!

A simple menu that works for us:

Breakfast
Coffee or cocoa and a Clif Bar (my favorite nutrition bar but there are a number of other brands).

Lunch
This is really more like a series of snacks throughout the day. Nuts, dried fruit, perhaps another Clif Bar. With lots and lots of water. Maybe with Tang.

Dinner
At night I want to relax and stuff my craw but I do not want to work at it. A freeze-dried dinner simmered in its own pouch by adding two cups of boiling water is my dream come true. Round it off with some chocolate for dessert and I'm there.

It's like this. I don't backpack to feast on gourmet or even good cooking. Satisfy the basic needs and your basic preferences. You'll probably be more than happy.

No stove, no cooking option
You don't need to cook to eat and drink properly. Eat the snack stuff listed under "Lunch" and drink water with or without flavoring. Think about it. No stove, no fuel, no cooking kit. No cooking, no clean-up. Less to pack and carry and less work.

Eating utensils
- Durable backpacking plastic cup with measurements on the side. Metal cups burn lips.
- Fork, spoon and (maybe) a knife. You can buy light, durable plastic ones at an outdoor store.
- Forget about dishes! Eat out of the cup, pot or freeze-dried pouch.

Cookware kit
Choose a kit that's durable, lightweight, compact and easy to clean. You can't beat stainless steel. Should

Simple kitchen: Durable plastic cups and eating utensils, small scrub sponges, biodegradable soap and cook kit.

come with a pot or two and a frying pan with a handle.

Cleaning Up

Clean up with a small scrubbing sponge and use biodegradable soap, if need be. Wash 50 feet or more from the stream or lake. Pack out the food scraps or bury them away from your site. Pack out all food packaging! Cans do not burn!

Basic nutrition

The food pyramid, from base to tip (you eat more from the groups at the base and less from those toward the tip):

A good basic cook kit: Stainless steel pots and pan with handles and lids. It tucks away like all good camping gear into a light, compact unit.

1. Carbohydrates – bread, pasta, cereal, grains.
2. Complex sugars, vitamins minerals – fruits and vegetables.
3. Dairy – milk, yogurt, cheese.
4. Protein – meat, poultry, fish, eggs.
5. Fats, sugars.

Carbohydrates (should comprise 40–50% of diet)
Include simple and complex sugars to fuel body. They contain four calories per gram.

Simple sugars are sucrose and fructose. They are commonly found in candies and desserts. Simple sugars provide quick bursts of energy.

Complex carbohydrates provide longer lasting sources of energy and are very important to outdoors people. Found in pasta, baked goods made of whole grains, rice and corn.

Proteins (should comprise 30–40% of your diet)
Known as the "building blocks" of nutrition. Especially important for children or those recovering from illness or injury. Protein comes from meat, fish, eggs, peanuts and soybeans. Canned or dried meat (like beef jerky) are ideal for backpacking. Four calories per gram.

Fats (should comprise less than 30% of your diet)
Fats are found in plant and animal oils. They produce that wonderful feeling of fullness. Fats are the most difficult of foods for the body to convert into energy. Fats are especially good for cold weather hiking since they are a whopping nine calories per gram.

Note: Fats and proteins require more oxygen to burn than carbs. At higher altitudes (where oxygen is in short supply) you may need that oxygen for straining muscles.

Calories and food weight
Backpacking may burn 4,000-5,000 calories a day. Street walking burns 300 calories per hour. Roughly figure 2–2.25 pounds of food to get 4,000 calories of energy.

Sample meals
Most of these items are available in a typical food store.

Dayhikes
Sandwiches of all sorts, cheese and crackers, dried fruit, granola and/or energy bars.

Overnights
Breakfast
- Make cold cereal by mixing dried milk and water and pouring it over granola or muesli. Or add boiling water to instant oatmeal or cream of wheat. Add dried fruit.
- Instant breakfast
- Breakfast bars
- Dried eggs

Lunch
Snack on this stuff during the day. Avoid eating one heavy meal in the middle of your trek.
- Dried fruit
- Granola
- Peanuts
- Chocolate chips
- Carob chips
- M&Ms
- Trail mix
- Nutrition bars (granola, Clif Bars, Power Bars)
- Crackers and cheese (cheese is OK for days at a time in your pack)
- Sandwiches of peanut butter with jam or honey
- Hard salami
- Sardines
- Canned fish or meat on crush-resistant bread like pita

All you need to prepare freeze-dried meals: Stove, pot and water. Boil the water, pour into the bag, let it simmer and eat out of the packaging. SImple, good.

Dinner

Make one-pot dinners using noodle-based or rice-based mixes. Or start with instant rice, instant potatoes or noodles, add dried milk, margarine (which will keep in a plastic container for days) freeze-dried vegetables, a small can of meat or dried cheese, mix in herbs and dried soup mixes to taste.

- Macaroni and cheese, noodle or rice dinners. Add small cans of meat and freeze-dried vegetables.
- Cook meat that defrosts in your pack.
- Heat up cans of stew, chili, tamales.

Dessert

- Instant pudding
- Candy bars
- Freeze-dried ice cream

Soup and drinks

- Dried soup
- Instant coffee
- Tea
- Cocoa
- Bouillon
- Tang

Freeze-dried (wondermeals!)

Freeze-dried backpacking food is surprisingly good, varied and easy to prepare. You just pour boiling water into the pouch it comes in and let it simmer for a few minutes. Eat it out of the same pouch! The advent of eatable, inexpensive freeze-dried food has begged the question: why cook?

STORY: Noodles and Snickers

Jonathan is a real mountain man. He spends his springs and summers hiking alone in the Sierras. His sister mails him food so he never has to leave the trail. She sends noodles and Snickers bars to outpost addresses that cater to hard-core backpackers like Jonathan. The noodles cost 20 cents a pound. I guess she gets a deal on the candy at Costco. I know what you're thinking, but he looked healthy when I met him. On that day he hiked up and down *two 12,000*-foot passes. So much for the food pyramid.

Parting words

- Eat things you don't have to cook, like energy bars and trail mix.
- Cook items that require little preparation or clean-up like prepackaged, freeze-dried dinners.
- Energy bars and trail mix are found in most food stores. Freeze-dried backpacking meals are available through outdoor stores, catalogs or online.

Labels to look for:

Cooksets
Coleman
Open Country
Peak 1
MSR

Freeze-dried food
AlpineAire
Backpacker's Pantry
Mountain House
Natural High

Mail order
REI: 800-426-4840 or www.rei.com
Campmor: 800-226-7667 or www.campmor.com

Price tags
Cooksets $13–35*
Freeze dried-dinners, two servings $5–7

*Price ranges are approximate.

Like a bizarre insect coming out of its pod and spreading its wings, this fairly typical type of backpacking stove is a curious gizmo.

When it works its hot blue flame really cooks. But many a hiker has cursed the courting period these tiny stoves sometimes demand.

Chapter Eleven:

Stoves

Backpacking stoves are tricky little gadgets and I have not the same faith or regard for them as I do for modern tents and water filters. Stoves are great once you have mastered one, but the road to mastery can be frustrating. On the other hand, cooking over an open fire is a challenging throwback to self-reliant woodsmanship. It can also be a lot more difficult than dealing with a backpacking stove.

The case against campfire cooking

Fires are often prohibited because:
- They leave an ugly mess.
- Wood is removed that would otherwise enrich the soil.
- There may be a fire hazard.
- They encourage irresponsible wood gathering.

Even if you may build fires you must deal with:
- Smoke
- Ashes
- Blackened pots
- Sparks
- Finding suitable (dry & hard) wood

In general it's more difficult and slower to cook over hot coals than a stove.

This setup will usually boil water in four minutes. With most freeze-dried meals that means you'll be eating in 15. That definitely beats cooking over a campfire.

The case for campfires

- Fires are fun.
- No uncooperative backpacking stove to kick and curse.
- Cooking successfully over a good bed of coals is a genuine challenge and builds character.
- It makes you feel like you're *Home, Home on the Range!*

Backpacking stoves

Stoves are categorized by the type of fuel they burn. Which is best? The one that works! They're all designed to fold and fit compactly in a backpack. If you're a tinkering type, you'll love these gadgets.

White gas
Hot flame, easy fuel to find, can be difficult to start.

Kerosene
Hot flame, even harder to start, easy fuel to find. Awful, smelly stuff.

Multi-fuel
Can burn two or more petroleum based liquid fuels (white gas, gasoline, kerosene).

Canister
Uses pressurized butane or propane gas. Easy to use, not as hot as white gas, but adjustable to simmer. May not work below freezing (blended fuels work in temperatures down in the teens). More expensive. May work better at lower temperatures in high altitudes. Used canisters must be packed out.

Alcohol stoves
Uncommon outside of Scandinavia. Flame not as hot as other fuels.

Like a car
Buy a stove. It's the sure-fire way to guarantee hot food and drink outdoors.

Buy a stove that you know how to work easily. Do not leave the store until you're 100% certain you do.

Practice lighting it at home. At the end of a day's hike you want to produce a hot blue flame almost at will. It's like a car. You want to turn the key and go!

Cooking over a campfire

You don't cook over flames. The best heat emanates from coals. A fire must be built and allowed to burn down to a bed of red hot coals. The better the wood (hard and dry, not rotten or wet) the better the coals. The bigger the fire, the more coals you'll have. Not that you need all that much — at it's peak, the flames should come up to your knees. No bonfires!

You can start a fire with firestarter or fuel from your stove, but the real scout starts a fire with one match. Find a handful of dry, brittle twigs and build a tepee in the fire ring. Determine which way the wind is blowing and add slightly larger pieces of wood on the opposite side of the tepee (you want the flame blowing into the wood). The trick is to use very thin twigs and sticks at this point. The right kind snap crisply when you bend them. Gather ever larger pieces of wood and have them ready to add as the fire grows.

Get down close. Light the match and stick the flame underneath and inside your little tepee. If the wind doesn't decide to play tricks, your dry, brittle twigs will catch immediately and spread to the larger stuff. After that it's just a matter of adding bigger sticks to the fire until bingo! you've got a full fire. Let the flames subside until all that remains are glowing coals. It may take around 45 minutes.

Rest the pot or pan directly on a flat, stable area of the coals if you can. Otherwise you can make a setting area with rocks. The trick is to cook over red hot coals without burning yourself or tipping over the pot or pan. If you're simply boiling water, heating something or preparing a quick-cook item (like trout or a potato patty made from an instant mix) this isn't too difficult. It may take 10–15 minutes to boil water.

Cooking over a fire is not a bad thing to know if that fancy stove doesn't work. But for reasons already listed, campfires are difficult to cook over and environmentally unsound. It's not recommended.

STORY: Molotov Cocktail

I have one of those backpacking stoves that must be primed just so before you can see that all-important blue flame. You pump it up, turn the dial until some white gas fills up a teeny dish underneath the burner, turn the dial off and then you light the dish. *Whoosh!* it goes and then you let the flame die down. Just before it does, you turn the dial back on and if the stars are in your favor, a steady, strong blue flame appears and you're on your way to outdoor cooking glory.

It's the *Whoosh!* part that stymies some chefs and concerns firefighters everywhere. Sometimes the gas overflows the dish and the start-up flame burns a hole in the ground. When I practiced with it at home I left three charred craters in my back yard. Since you're sticking your face down there when you light it, eyebrows tend to disappear. The thought that you might be completely blown away crosses your mind when you see the two-foot flame engulf the attached fuel bottle. The explosive nature of the "priming" process has prompted one backpacking friend to call these stoves the camper's molotov cocktail.

Parting words
- Buy or rent a name brand backpacking stove that you know how to work.
- Give yourself plenty of daylight to fiddle. Make camp well before dark.

Labels to look for
Liquid Fuel
MSR
Peak 1
Primus Multi-Fuel
Trangia

Solid Fuel
ZZ Sierra Zip

Canister/butane and propane
Gaz
Peak 1
Primus Multi-Fuel

Mail order
REI: 800-426-4840 or www.rei.com
Campmor: 800-226-7667 or www.campmor.com

Price tag
Backpacking stove $25–99*

Renting
Backpacking stove $6–12 first day
$2–4 each additional day
$50 deposit

*Price ranges are approximate.

Chapter Twelve:

Toilet

Unfortunately, there aren't many trail-side toilet facilities in the back country.

Here's an amusing thought. It's recommended to practice everything at home before your first hike. Set up the tent, light the stove and so forth. I wonder if I should be the very first to recommend that novices dig a latrine in their back yards and practice the woodsman's squat. It does take some practice.

Believe it or not, urinating isn't a sanitation problem. Just pee away and out of sight. Please.

The other takes a procedure and some getting used to. Get at least 200 feet away from the lake or stream. Dig a small hole around six inches deep with a piece of bark or a small plastic trowel. Squat and go. Cover with the dirt you dug up and make it look like you never said hello.

Wipe if you wish with your toilet paper, wrap the used with some fresh and insert in a Ziploc bag.

Do not bury. Foraging animals will not allow TP to stay buried. Once dug up it often blows up onto a nearby bush for the next hiker to admire.

Do not burn. Used TP is not very combustible and it can be messy trying. Folks often give up and leave their surprises for the next camper.

It's best to carry it out. Just find a secret, secluded place for it in your pack and forget it's there until you need to remember again.

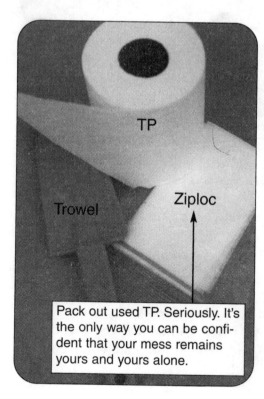

TP

Trowel

Ziploc

Pack out used TP. Seriously. It's the only way you can be confident that your mess remains yours and yours alone.

Clearing the bowels in an outdoor setting can be a mental thing. Some folks are very skittish about squatting, wiping and packing it up (no clean white bowl and seat, no dainty wipe-wipe, no rushing water). The utter rawness is overwhelming. Shy ones may even become constipated. Oh dear.

Toilet kit: Biodegradable soap (works on pots and pans, too), DEET, sun block, packaged towelettes, small towel, toothbrush, toothpaste, TP and trowel.

Think quick and clean. Like you're clearing the mud from your boots. It's OK. It's natural. Ziploc and carry out used tampons, too.

General bathing
Wash up with plain water or with biodegradable soap at least 100 feet from the stream or lake.

Same with brushing teeth.

STORY: Beware the Bum Bug

Toilet stories are easy. My wife's first attempt with a trench was dismal. After 21 minutes of fussing she came back with a wad of toilet paper the size of a basketball. It took her ten minutes to psych up, one minute to let loose and ten minutes to wipe. Guess who had to deal with the basketball.

It's all in your head, I said.

I was afraid that a bug was going to crawl up my bum, she said.

Was anything resolved? I guess: Some are never meant to enjoy or even endure the latrine hop.

Parting words
● Dig, squat, wipe, Ziploc, bury. Don't be such a baby!

Outdoor safety & well-being

There is always concern in guides of this sort about safety. There should be. Especially important is the need to stay hydrated and to have immediate access to drinkable water at all times. Equally important is the need and capability to stay warm and dry. Finally, someone not on the hike must know your hiking plans (where and when you're starting, where you're going, where and when you're ending).

> **Water + Warm & Dry + Leaving Word = Basic Well-being**

However, it's not the lost planet out there. There's stuff to know in order to maintain well-being but how's that much different than knowing how to drive an automobile safely on a freeway?

The following subjects are in alphabetical order:

Altitude
As you hike higher there is less and less oxygen. At 10,000 feet there is 30% less oxygen than at sea level. This can be a problem for those who live at lower levels hiking up to 7,000 feet or higher.

Take one or two days to acclimate at the higher level without strenuous exercise. Then take it easy the first day. Climb no more than 1,000 feet a day after that. For every 3,000-foot gain take a day of rest. Increase your fluid and carbohydrate intake. Keep in mind that fats and proteins take more oxygen to metabolize — oxygen you may need for laboring body parts!

Altitude Sickness

Acute mountain sickness (AMS) is the most common illness associated with altitude. It can begin from 7,000–9,000 feet if one is not acclimatized. Symptoms include nausea, dizziness, loss of appetite, headache and weakness. Stop to acclimate, or for immediate relief descend 1,000–3,000 feet. If you are susceptible, a doctor can prescribe drugs.

When AMS becomes severe, two life-threatening conditions may result:

High-altitude pulmonary edema (HAPE) is indicated by extreme shortness of breath, the need to sit up to breathe, coughing and the inability to sleep.

High-altitude cerebral edema (HACE) is indicated by severe headache, vomiting, confusion, loss of balance and coordination and loss of consciousness.

In both cases, the victim must be taken to a lower altitude immediately. The conditions progress rapidly and death can result.

Bandits (protecting your parked car from two- and four-legged criminals)

Disable your car by removing the rotor and/or distributor cap. Lock the fuel cap. Bears can literally dismantle an auto looking for stuff to eat (yes, they can!). Remove food and make sure nothing inside looks like a cooler. Lock and shut windows and doors.

Bears

If you run into a bear, more than likely it'll be a black bear. It will not eat you. However, black bears have learned that humans are an excellent source for food and they will make attempts to get at your stash. They are active day and night at all altitudes.

● Make noise as you hike. Bears are shy and will avoid you.

● You are responsible for protecting food from bears. Open food encourages the development of a "problem bear" (one that stalks campers and their food). Such animals must eventually be killed.

● In camp, store food and all odoriferous items such as toothpaste and scented soap in bear boxes or bear canisters. Canisters hold three–five days worth of food and weigh three–five pounds empty. They are rigid and bulky in your pack. Bear boxes are better. Or hang your items by counterbalancing (see directions next page).

● When dayhiking from base camp where you can't bear-box food, take the food with you.

● Scare curious bears away immediately. Jump up and down, wave your arms and make noise (bang pots, blow a whistle, set off a hand-held fog horn).

When confronted with bears or mountain lions make yourself tall and make a lot of noise. Do not run! Alan has wisely chosen Alison to lead the counterattack. Kennison the dog is guarding the rear.

● Do not battle a bear for food already taken. You will not win. Neither will you starve to death in the three-four days it takes to get back to base camp. Before you nod off, unzip pack pockets so bears don't rip them off looking for snacks.

● Don't take food into your tent or sleeping bag! A bear will crawl in there with you.

● Store garbage the same as food. Clean up thoroughly. Pack your garbage out!

Counterbalancing (when there isn't a bear box)

● Find a tree with a live branch you can throw a rock over (at least 25 feet high).

● Divide food into two equal sacks (8–10 pounds each) or counterbalance food with a sack of rocks.

● Tie a rock to the end of a strong, thin rope and toss it over the branch. Position rope on that part of branch that will support food but not a bear cub (about 10 feet from trunk).

● Tie pots or cups to one bag to act as noisemakers.

● Tie the first sack to the end of the rope and hoist it over the branch.

● Tie the other sack to the other end of the rope as high as you can. Place excess rope in the sack and leave a loop for retrieval.

● With a stick push the second sack up until it's at the same height as the first sack. Sacks should be well out of reach (about 12 feet high).

● To retrieve, push one sack until the other descends to where you can reach it.

● Make sure you hold the other end of the rope as you detach one of the bags.

● Sleep close enough to the setup so if a bear comes you can scare it away.

● Above the tree line use a rock overhang or the stash-in-a-crack method (you can retrieve the food but a heavy-pawed bear cannot).

Blisters

When you first feel the hot spot, bandage and/or pad it with moleskin. If it's already a blister, lance it with a sterile needle (just run the needle through a match flame) and bandage. Make sure your bandage is secure.

Often the pounding and flexing of your feet will lift the bandage from the affected area. If you treat and pad blisters soon enough you might be OK for the rest of the hike, unless shoes are a poor fit to begin with.

Pack a first aid guide just in case.

First Aid
Discuss possible emergency situations with your hiking partners. Pack a first-aid guide. First-aid kits often come with such information. See **first aid information** in "Resources."

Heat Exhaustion and Heatstroke
Heat exhaustion comes on gradually over a day or several days. Symptoms include fatigue and weakness. The victim feels bad but can still perspire. Get him out of the sun, have him drink fluids and rest.

Heatstroke is much more dangerous and attacks quickly. Breathing becomes short and labored. Muscles feel like they're on fire. The victim suffers blurred vision, dizziness and nausea. Sweating ceases and his body temperature soars. The body's cooling mechanism shuts down and consciousness is lost. The victim needs shade, fluids and rest. Cool the body by pouring liquids over the victim or by immersing him in a water source.

Prevention, of course, is best. Always drink before you're thirsty. Dehydration is indicated by lack of urinating or dark urine. Avoid caffeine and alcohol since they activate the kidneys resulting in fluid loss.

Hypothermia

This is the most deadly hazard to hikers. Subnormal body temperature is caused by exposure to cold, and intensified by wetness, wind and fatigue. First symptoms are uncontrollable shivering and imperfect motor coordination followed by loss of judgment. Prevention is key. Stay dry. Carry wind and rain protection and put it on as soon as the weather dictates. Stay warm. Wear wool or suitable synthetic (not cotton) against your skin.

If the weather gets bad and you're unprepared, flee or hunker down. Protect yourself and remain as warm and dry as possible.

Treat shivering at once. Hypothermia acts quickly and disables the victim's ability to judge his condition. Get the victim out of the wind and rain. Replace all wet clothes with dry, put him in a sleeping bag and keep him awake. Give him warm drinks. No booze. For severe shivering, strip the victim down and warm him with other naked bodies wrapped in a sleeping bag.

Lightning

Seek thick woods away from the tallest trees. Avoid being the highest object in a 50-foot radius. Avoid mountain ridges, open meadows, lone trees, shallow caves or the base or edge of cliffs. Get rid of metal objects (like your pack frame). If you're in an exposed place, put insulating material (sleeping pad or poncho) on a small rock and sit on it. Clasp knees and touch rock with feet and buttocks only.

Losing Your Way
Prevention
Use a good map. Bring a compass. Stay on the trails. Remember prominent landmarks and evaluate distances to and from them as you hike. Keep track of the sun's position.

Lost
Stay in a clearing or large rocky outcropping. Lay out a colorful tarp or build a small smoky fire in a safe area. Find protection from the wind (tent, boulders, log or hollow). Stay put. Dress warmly before you get cold. Wrap in a space blanket or poncho. Huddle with others upon a ground cover. Don't panic.

Mosquitoes and Biting Bugs
Use a repellent containing N, N diethylmeta-toluamide (DEET) and you should be OK. Wear clothing that covers skin. A funky head net with a snug neckband works wonders with swarming bugs.

Mountain Lions
Pick up small children. Don't run. Don't hide. Stand tall. Hold your ground. Wave hands, shout, throw sticks and rocks. If attacked fight back.

Poison Oak and Poison Ivy
Not always easy to spot. Remember this rhyme: Leaves of three, let it be. If you think you've brushed against these plants, wash with soap and water.

Rattlesnakes
Most common around riverbeds and streams under 7000 feet. Bite is rarely fatal. You may want to carry a snake bite kit called Extractor. If you hear the rattle, determine its location and detour.

Stream Crossings
If there's no better crossing and turning back is not an option:

Wait until morning when the level is lowest. Rig a rope over the stream if possible. Unfasten the hip belt of your pack in case you have to free yourself from it. Keep your boots (or some sort of footwear with traction) on. Don't face downstream as your legs may buckle from the current. Move your foot only when the other is secure. Don't cross your legs. Use a stick for support.

Ticks
DEET works on ticks, too. Check yourself often and watch where you sit. Pull ticks straight out with tweezers being careful not to leave the head. The Dog Tick is big enough to see easily. The Deer Tick is very small and may carry Lyme disease.

Ultraviolet Rays
The sun's rays become stronger with elevation. Cover exposed skin, wear sunglasses and a hat with a visor.

STORY: That's OK. You go ahead.
I guess I'm lucky. I've never been hurt on the trail. I've been woozy and nauseated from dehydration and altitude sickness, suffered cramped and blistered feet, all

---

Two diseases spread by ticks

If you get ill after a hike, see a doctor. Both of the following illnesses can be treated with antibiotics.

Lyme Disease

Indications include a bull's-eye red rash around the bite that appears 3–30 days after the attack. Also flu-like symptoms including muscle aches, fever, fatigue and nausea. Lyme disease can cause serious neurological and arthritic complications.

Rocky Mountain Spotted Fever

An eastern United States malady with a 2–14 day incubation. Symptoms include fever and a red-spotted rash on hands and feet spreading to torso. It can be fatal.

---

sorts of minor discomforts like sleepless nights and sore joints as well as the mental anguish of domestic quarreling — but nothing close to serious.

When I was a boy I once broke my finger the first day of summer camp and for two weeks suffered a very swollen and painful appendage. The first-aid guy thought it was a sprain or something. On my very first camping trip as a boy scout I cut my finger the first night of a weekend trip carving a neckerchief slide. It was a nasty little slice that never got stitched (I spent the weekend out there) and to this day is slightly lumpy from scar tissue.

What I consider luck is probably influenced by the increased sense of safety that maturity brings. I didn't take up serious hiking and backpacking until I was an adult. When you're older, you don't feel the intense desire to leap off or climb up dangerous places. If it's do-able and fun, yes (I'm not a total wuss), but to prove my manhood, no. The latter is really a guy thing and happens when guys get together and decide to be irrational, foolhardy and stupid.

My favorite wayward manhood rite wasn't exactly a hiking accident. It was a mountain biking accident but it illustrates a point. A bunch of fellows went biking in the desert back country of San Diego, California, and it should be noted that most were weekend warriors at best. I didn't go because I knew some of the personalities involved and I knew what was going to happen. Instead of staying on the trails they all decided to take a deep plunge down a steep rocky gorge. It's something you can do on a mountain bike, of course, if you have the expertise. I've made a hair-raising run or two myself, but my craving for split-second, near-death experiences have given way to challenges colored by pleasure and physical effort.

Well, two of the most talented (and headstrong) riders tumbled and crashed into cactus, breaking bones and covering themselves with thousands of sharp spines. They were several miles back and what saved the accidents from turning into a full blown crisis was the fact that most of the riders were firefighters highly trained in emergency first aid. They knew what to do and got the victims to hospitals quickly. I was told it took two hours for one guy to have all the cactus needles plucked from his body.

The point? Safety and well-being is often a hiker's rational choice. It's not likely that a freak lightning bolt or an enraged mother bear will harm you on your next trip. It's your own highly tuned sense of well-being that will keep you sound and pull you through when you need it.

Parting words
● Use your head!

Labels to look for
First-aid kits
Adventure Medical Kits
Atwater Carey

Books
Wilderness and Travel Medicine by Eric A. Weiss, M.D.

Mail order
REI: 800-426-4840 or www.rei.com
Campmor: 800-226-7667 or www.campmor.com

Price tag
First-aid kits $19–75*

*Price ranges are approximate.

Chapter Fourteen:

Maps

It's wise to hike with a good map of the area you're traveling. Learn how to follow it and to match it with your surroundings. That's all you'll need for most hiking areas including state and national parks as well as U.S. Forest Service Lands.

Maps

Chances are your first hikes will be over mapped, well-used trails in local, state or national parks or national forests. Such trails often have plenty of signs pointing the way, but it's wise to carry a good map.

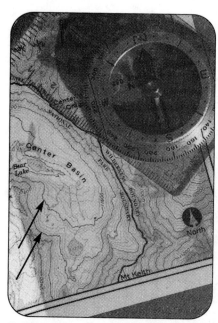

Contour maps indicate elevations. Contour lines are all the squiggly lines that spread like concentric circles around hills and mountains. The contours will give you an idea of what you're in for — bunched up lines means it's gonna be steep, widely spaced lines indicate easier going.

The best have contour lines that show the lay of the land based on USGS (U.S. Geological Survey) topographical maps. At a glance you can determine where the trail crosses steep terrain (several contour lines close together) or a gently sloping meadow (contour lines widely spaced).

Good maps have a legend or directory that indicates which way is north and defines the colors, lines and symbols used in the map. Here is where you'll find the scale of the map and how many feet or meters of change each contour line represents.

Using a map

It's important to feel comfortable with a map and to develop a sense of direction with one. Look up and examine the lay of the land around you. Identify landmarks such as lakes, mountaintops or hilltops as well as your trail. Spread the map out and find those landmarks on the map. **Align the map to what you are seeing**

and to the trail you're on. You should be able to approximate where you are on the trail. This is how most hikers find their way around.

To find trails and maps of trails look under **Finding Trails** in the resource section.

Compass

Using a compass is easy if you believe the instructional books, but in truth the finer points of navigation can be challenging to some of us. If you remain on the trail in an established outdoor area, carry a map and know how to read it, you're not going to get lost.

A compass can come in handy in special circumstances — like coming upon an unmapped fork in the trail or becoming lost in a deep fog. Knowing where magnetic north lies (the direction pointed out by the needle in the compass) can be enough to steer you in the right direction.

Some find compass navigation interesting and helpful. If you're not using an established trail system you better know how to use a compass. Suggested reading includes *The Essential Wilderness Navigator* by David Seidman and *Be Expert with Map and Compass* by Bjorn Kjellstrom.

Parting words

● Hike with a map and know how to use one.

Chapter Fifteen:

Backpacker's list

Basic Equipment
Backpack
Tent with rain fly
Ground cloth or tarp
Sleeping bag
Sleeping pad

Emergency Essentials
Water (one quart)
Emergency clothing (rain gear and pullover)
Flashlight and batteries
Emergency food (energy bars)
First-aid kit:
There are complete kits available with first-aid guides.
  A very basic kit includes:
  Antiseptic cleanser
  Bandages
  Tape
  Gauze pads
  Aspirin or pain relievers
  Moleskin
  Towelettes
  Scissors
  Tweezers
Compass and map
Candle and matches
Pocket knife (a Swiss Army knife is best)
Whistle
Emergency shelter (tarp or space blanket)

Water purification system or iodine
Sunglasses

Clothing
(Season will dictate)
Hiking boots
Socks and liners
Shorts
Pants
Shirts
Pullovers
Rain gear
Hat

Kitchen & Eating Supplies
Water purification system
Stove and fuel
Cook kit (pot with lid, pot gripper and frying pan)
Utensils for eating and cooking
Drinking cups (for eating, too. Plastic is best.)
Water containers (for washing)
Paper towels
Trash bags with closers

Toilet Supplies
All-purpose biodegradable soap (for kitchen, too)
Toothbrush (and toothpaste if desired)
Towelettes
Small cloth towel
Insect repellent
Sun block
Toilet paper
Latrine trowel

Other
Extra glasses
Backpacking lantern
Nylon cord (50–100 ft.)
Stuff bags
Fishing gear and license

Food
Energy bars
Trail mix
Freeze-dried meals
Instant noodle or rice-based meals

Summary of Costs

Boots	$45–200*
Sock liners	$3
Socks	$6
Underwear, crew	$16–45
Underwear, pants	$16–37
Insulating layer, pullover	$30–70
Insulating layer, pants	$30–98
Outer shell, parka	$80–389
Outer shell, pants	$40–295
Shorts	$17–40
Pants	$27–72
Rain gear, jacket	$29–59
Rain gear, pants	$15–39
Rain gear, poncho	$5
Hat	$10–35
Gloves	$12–50
Sunglasses	$16–80
External-frame pack	$120–190
Internal-frame pack	$175–300
Daypacks	$30–55
Down mummy sleeping bag	$170–440
Synthetic mummy sleeping bag	$120–305
Closed cell sleeping pad	$12–25
Self-inflating mattress	$45–105
Bag liners	$29–107
Two-person tent	$89–275
Bivy	$150–275
Water Filters	$35–275
Water Purifiers	$70–130
Cook sets	$13–35
Freeze-dried dinners	$5–7 (serves two)

Backpacking stove	$25–99
First-aid kits	$19–75

Renting

External-frame pack	$10–20 first day $5–10 each additional day $50 deposit
Internal-frame pack	$15–25 first day $5–10 each additional day $50 deposit
Sleeping bag	$10–30 first day, $6–12 each additional day, $50 deposit
Sleeping pads	$ 5–17 first day, $1–6 each additional day, $50 deposit
Two-person tent	$15–25 first day, $5–10 each additional day, $50 deposit
Backpacking stove	$ 6–12 first day, $2–4 each additional day, $50 deposit

*Price ranges are approximate.

Making sense of the costs

You can rent packs, sleeping bags and pads, tent and stove for about $150 for two days. That leaves boots, clothing, cook set, food and the rest of the list. Boots are a major purchase, around $150 or so. Warm weather gear you probably have. A good cook set costs about $35. Food is not expensive and the rest of the list can be jury-rigged or ignored for your first gentle foray into the woods. So you'll invest between $300–350 dollars just to see if you like backpacking this summer. A lot? Well, maybe.

Here's the thing. You can buy the major stuff you need for summer trips for $800–$1,000 and most of the stuff will last a lifetime. For each trip you take thereafter the only cost is food, permits, stove fuel and gas. Initial costs are rather high if you have none of the gear, but once you have it, backpacking is one of the cheaper ways to enjoy an active lifestyle.

So to simply *try* the pursuit of backpacking, it helps to **borrow** stuff. If you can't borrow, **rent what you must and jury-rig the rest.** Then if you want to pursue it and make even just one trip a year, spend the money. It's a value over the long haul. Not to mention all the rewarding experiences you're going to have!

Glossary

Acclimation: Getting the body to get used to (or to acclimate) to higher elevation through gradual and controlled exposure.

DEET: The active ingredient in popular and effective insect repellents (N,N-diethyl-meta-toluamide).

External frame: The outside supporting frame of a backpack.

Giardia lamblia: A protozoan found in animal and human feces that causes serious intestinal illness if ingested.

Hypothermia: Extremely low core body temperature. One of the greatest outdoor dangers.

Internal frame: Refers to the supporting stays built into a backpack.

Loft: A sleeping bag's ability to fluff up, trap air and insulate.

Moleskin: The sticky-backed padding used to cover blisters and hot spots.

Mummy bag: A tapered sleeping bag preferred by backpackers.

Rain fly: A waterproof tent covering.

Space blanket: A sheet of aluminized mylar. Reflective

silver on one side and orange on the other. Used as an emergency wrap or shelter. Wind- and waterproof.

Switchbacks: The zig-zagging trails that reduce the steepness of a hiker's climb up a hill or mountain.

Topographic map: A map that explains the lay of the land through contour lines that indicate elevation.

Trail head: That spot off a main road that indicates the start of a trail.

Tree line: That elevation where trees no longer grow.

Resources

Outdoor clothing and gear

Stores

Until you know what you're looking for you probably shouldn't order through the mail or on-line. Besides, there is nothing like checking out the goods in a quality outdoor store. It's seeing and feeling. Stores that really cater to outdoor needs help build your enthusiasm to get out there!

REI

Of the mass merchants, REI is king. They do not sell baseball bats or yo-yos. It's the true outdoorperson's store. There are over 50 REIs across the country. The gear is great and reasonably priced. The help is friendly, knowledgeable and experienced. You can rent gear here, too.

Other mass merchants don't carry as great a variety of top-notch outdoor merchandise. Often tents, backpacks, sleeping bags and clothing may look the part, but materials and craftsmanship are lacking.

In towns without a nearby REI, there will probably be a retailer who carries the right stuff. See the lists of name brands to look for at the end of the chapters

To locate an REI near you on the web go to www.rei.com.

Campmor

They don't have a lot of stores, but they have a delicious mail order catalog. Like REI, the gear is good and the prices can't be beat. Website and 800 number are listed below.

On-line catalogs and ordering
www.rei.com
www.campmor.com
www.lands end.com (clothing)
www.llbean.com

Mail order catalogs and ordering
REI 800-426-4840
Campmor 800-226-7667
Lands End 800-356-4444
llbean.com 800-221-4221

Quality brands
To find out more about the brands that are listed after certain chapters in this book log on to these sites:

www.the backpacker.com/company.html

www.bpbasecamp.com/vendor

outside.starwave.com:80/outsidestore/index.html

www.outdoorlink.com/outdoor.products.html

On-line hiking and backpacking information
www.gorp.com
A general wealth of outdoor information.

www.bpbasecamp.com
Backpacker Magazine.

www.thebackpacker.com

www.greatoutdoors.com/hiking/index.htm

www.adventuresports.com

outside.starwave.com:80
Outside Magazine. Especially helpful is Gear Guy.

www.outdoorlink.com

www.hikenet.com
Includes a listing of hiking and outdoor clubs.

www.trailshead.com

Hiking and backpacking books
Backpacking: Woman's Guide by Adrienne Hall (1998)

Advanced Backpacking: A Trailside Guide by Karen Berger (1998)

The Backpacker's Field Manual: A Comprehensive Guide to Mastering Backcountry Skills by Rick Curtis (1998)

The Backpacker's Handbook by Chris Townsend (1996)

Backpacking in the 90s: Tips, Techniques & Secrets by Victoria Logue (1995)

Backpacking Made Easy by Michael Abel (1975)

Backpacking, One Step at a Time by Harvey Manning (1986)

The Basic Essentials of Backpacking by Harry Roberts (1989)

The Camper's and backpacker's Bible by Thoma E. Huggler (1995)

Camping and Backpacking with Children by Steven Boga (1995)

Everyday Wisdom: 1,001 Expert Tips for Hikers by Karen Berger (1997)

A Hiker's Companion: 12,000 Miles of Trail-Tested Wisdom by Cindy Ross (1993)

Hiking and Backpacking by Eric Seaborg and Ellen Dudley (1994)

Check these websites for books as well:
www.amazon.com
Search Backpacking. Bingo!

www.falconguide.com

<u>Magazines about hiking and backpacking</u>
Backpacker
Rodale Press, Inc.
33 East Minor Street
Emmaus, PA 18098
610-967-5171

Fax 610-967-8181
Website: www.bpbasecamp.com

Outside
400 Market Street
Sante Fe, NM 87501
505-989-7100
Website: http://outside.starwave.com

First aid information
Look in the resource section of your Yellow Pages. Bet you didn't even know it was there! Look up your local American Red Cross for classes.

First aid books:
A Comprehensive Guide to Wilderness & Travel Medicine by Eric A. Weiss, M.D.

Medicine for the Outdoors by Paul S. Auerbach, M.D.

Wilderness Medicine by William Forgey, M.D.

Medicine for Mountaineering and Other Wilderness Activities by James A. Wilkerson, M.D.

Finding trails
National Park Service
Department of the Interior
1849 C Street NW, Room 1013
Washington DC 20240
www.nps.gov/parks.html

U.S. Forest Service
Department of Agriculture
14th Street and Independence Avenue SW
Washington, DC 20250
www.fs.fed.us/recreation

Bureau of Land Management
Department of the Interior
1849 C Street NW
Washington, DC 20240

www.outdoorlink.com/amtrails/resources/state-trails/index.html

www.gorp.com/gorp/resource/main.htm

www.thebackpacker.com/dest/trails.html

Bibliography

Backpacker. Emmaus, Pennsylvania: Rodale Press, Inc., 10-1997.

Berger, Karen. Hiking & Backpacking: A Complete Guide. New York, New York: W.W. Norton & Company, 1995.

Crapsey, Malinee. Backcountry Basics. Three Rivers, California: United States Department of the Interior, 5-19-98.

Fletcher, Colin. The Complete Walker. New York, New York: Alfred A. Knopf, 1998.

Hall, Adrienne. A Ragged Mountain Press Woman's Guide: Backpacking. Camden, Maine: Ragged Mountain Press, 1998.

Saldana, Lori. Backpacking Primer. La Crescenta, California: Mountain N'Air Books, 1995.

Seaborg, Eric. Hiking and Backpacking. Champaign, Illinois: Human Kinetics, 1994.

Steidman, David. The Essential Navigator. Camden, Maine: Ragged Mountain Press, 1995.

Stienstra, Tom. California Camping. San Francisco, California: Foghorn Press, 1987.

Time. New York, New York: Time, Inc., 10-26-1998.

UC Berkeley Wellness Letter. Berkeley, California:
University of California at Berkeley, 12-1998.

Winnett, Thomas. Sierra South. Berkeley, California:
Wilderness Press, 1993.

Index

About the Author & Start-Up Sports

Doug Werner is the author of all ten books in the *Start-Up Sports Series*. He has been interviewed on CNN and numerous radio talk shows throughout the United States. His books have appeared on ESPN, been featured in prominent national publications, and sold throughout the United States, Canada, Great Britain and Japan.

The series celebrates the challenge of learning a new sport with emphasis on basic technique, safety and fun. Imbued with a unique beginner's perspective, *Start-Up* books explain and explore what it's really like to learn.

Each book has the endorsement of prominent individuals, publications and organizations in each respective sport including Steve Hawk of *Surfer Magazine*, Ted Martin of International Snowboard Federation, Chuck Nichols of America's Cup 1995, *Bowler's Journal, Longboarder Magazine, Ski Magazine, Snow Country, Veteran Fencer's Quarterly*. The series has received critical acclaim from *Booklist, Library Journal, Outside Kids, Boys Life, The San Francisco Examiner* and *The Orange County Register.*

Werner is a graduate of Cal State Long Beach and holds a degree in fine arts. In previous life times he established a graphics business in 1980, an advertising agency in 1984 and yet another graphics business in 1987. By 1993 he had decided to move on and began writing sport instructional guides. In 1994 he established Tracks Publishing and the *Start-Up Sports* series. Doug lives in San Diego, California with his wife Kathleen and daughter Joy.

Ordering More Start-Up Sports Books:

The Start-Up Sports series:

❑ Surfer's Start-Up
❑ Snowboarder's Start-Up
❑ Sailor's Start-Up
❑ In-line Skater's Start-Up
❑ Bowler's Start-Up

❑ Longboarder's Start-Up
❑ Golfer's Start-Up
❑ Fencer's Start-Up
❑ Boxer's Start-Up
❑ Backpacker's Start-Up

Each book costs $12.95 (includes priority postage)
Send a check for this amount to:

Tracks Publishing
140 Brightwood Avenue
Chula Vista, CA 91910

Or call 1-800-443-3570.
Visa and MasterCard accepted.

Start-Up Sports books are available in all major book-
stores and selected sporting goods stores.

www.startupsports.com

Start-Up Sports ®
celebrating the challenge

3 1191 00607 2573